It Is Well with My Soul

It Is Well with My Soul

Messages of Hope for the Bereaved

[signature: Harold T. Lewis]

Harold T. Lewis

Foreword by Richard A. Burnett

WIPF & STOCK · Eugene, Oregon

IT IS WELL WITH MY SOUL
Messages of Hope for the Bereaved

Wipf & Stock
An Imprint of Wipf and Stock Publishers
199 W. 8th Ave., Suite 3
Eugene, OR 97401

www.wipfandstock.com

PAPERBACK ISBN: 978-1-5326-5253-0
HARDCOVER ISBN: 978-1-5326-5254-7
EBOOK ISBN: 978-1-5326-5255-4

Manufactured in the U.S.A.   12/13/18

And, Lord, haste the day when the faith shall be sight,
The clouds be rolled back as a scroll,
The trump shall resound and the Lord shall descend,
"Even so," it is well with my soul.
It is well with my soul,
It is well, it is well with my soul.

Horatio Spafford (1828–1888)

In pia memoria matris meae amatissimae

MURIEL KATHLEEN WORRELL LEWIS

Contents

Foreword

THIS IS TRULY A mysterious book.

No, not in the sense of an Agatha Christie whodunit. Nor is it like a dense, jargon-riddled tome intended only for theologians. The mystery found in this book is the central claim of Christian living: the Paschal Mystery, "a cycle of rebirth," as Ronald Rolheiser says in his modern classic, *The Holy Longing*. It is "an invitation to live into the kingdom and reign of God . . . to see differently," in the words of liturgist Susan Marie Smith. In this collection of sermons (along with its extensive introduction), Harold Lewis unravels, in his own way, the Paschal Mystery and, in so doing, provides us with many lenses for clearer understanding of and more profound insights into the mystery of the life of Christ, which Jesus himself shared with his friends in those first peripatetic homilies offered throughout the Galilean countryside.

In the pages of *It Is Well with My Soul*, we meet over and over the Apostle Paul, who tells the Christians at Rome, "If we have died with Christ, we believe we shall also live with him" (Rom 6:8). For Lewis, Christian preaching should never be absent from Christian burial. Indeed, Dr. Lewis would have gotten along famously with a visiting professor of liturgics who proclaimed: "If the Christian church cannot speak at the time of death, it cannot speak at all." In these pages, too, we encounter not only Lewis the preacher and teacher but also Lewis the racial reconciler, Lewis the historian, and Lewis the pastor. For only the pastor can admonish his seminary flock: "Thou shalt not bleed on your congregation"—which I have always taken to mean that, in vague or clumsy attempts to seek the heights of what is often called narrative preaching, we must be careful not to confuse the subject of all preaching, Christ and Him crucified, with ourselves! As Paul reminds us, we must preach "not ourselves but Jesus Christ as Lord and ourselves as your servants for Jesus' sake" (2 Cor 4:5).

Harold Lewis, a devoted son of the Anglo-Catholic expression of Anglicanism, understands the role of liturgical preaching too well to expect the sermon to stand alone in the Burial Rite. For him, the sermon gives voice to the many other voices in prayer and recollection, grief and thanksgiving, humor and confession, and joyful songs raised to the Lord Jesus who, by his love alone, receives the departed "upon another shore and in a greater light." The Paschal Mystery is the heart of all Christian proclamation, and in this book we are given, even now, glimpses of "the blessing granted us through the prayers of many."

In these funeral sermons, preached at the memorial liturgies of the famous and not-so-famous over the past three decades, Dr. Lewis offers brave witness to the Resurrection and insights into the greatest mysteries we share as the Body of Christ. But whether preaching to the diocesan family of a bishop taken away from them in his one hundredth year, or to the parents, siblings, and friends of a young man who took his own life at thirty, Lewis—a man who has been a leader in Christian social witness and has lived at the center of the Episcopal Church's dynamic engagement in the world—sounds the clarion call of sure and certain hope with characteristic wit and wisdom. Thus inspired, the bereaved may leave worship proclaiming in their hearts and on their lips: "It is well with my soul."

Richard A. Burnett
Trinity Episcopal Church, Columbus, Ohio

Introduction

"Sure and certain hope"

I HAVE VIVID MEMORIES of participating in my Grandmother Edith's funeral when I was sixteen years old. The family—her five surviving children and their spouses, a dozen or so grandchildren, and an assortment of other kin—processed into the church, mournfully walking behind the coffin, and sat down in the front pews reserved for them. I, however, did not join them. When we arrived at the church, I reported to the sacristy, and asked the rector if I could be the acolyte for the service. One of my duties was to carry the ornate brass and mahogany processional cross before the coffin as we entered and as we left the church. After the funeral, I placed it in the hearse, alongside the coffin, and when we arrived at the cemetery, I retrieved the cross and led the body to its final resting place.

Now I don't think that the word "oxymoron" was in my vocabulary at the time, but had it been, I think I would have used it to describe what I heard next. As the priest took a clump of earth and traced with it the sign of the Cross on the coffin, he said: "Unto Almighty God we commend the soul of our sister departed, and we commit her body to the ground, earth to earth, ashes to ashes, dust to dust, in sure and certain hope of the Resurrection unto eternal life through our Lord Jesus Christ." To my young mind, something didn't click. To me, hope, by definition, was anything but sure and certain. Hope was an expression of something we would like to happen. We express a hope that it won't rain, so that we can go on a picnic; we hope that the girl in our class will go with us to the prom; we hope that Mother has made bread pudding for dessert. But there is nothing either sure or certain about those hopes. It might rain torrents, canceling the picnic. Our would-be date may already be spoken for. And Mother might serve us canned peaches because she didn't have time to make dessert.

But to the Christian, "sure and certain hope" is not an oxymoron at all. It is a statement of faith, not dependent upon our feeble wishes and desires. This is why the Apostle Paul assures the Romans: "Hope does not disappoint us, because God's love has been poured into our heart through the Holy Spirit" (Rom 5:5). This is why St. Peter can assure those under persecution with the words: "God has given us new birth into a living hope by the resurrection of Jesus Christ from the dead" (1 Pet 1:3). And this is why we can say with confidence at every funeral: "Jesus Christ, who rose victorious from the dead . . . comforts us with the blessed hope of everlasting life. For to your faithful people, O Lord, life is changed, not ended, and when our mortal body lies in death, there is prepared for us a dwelling-place eternal in the heavens."[1]

"Life is changed, not ended." In other words, eternal life is not something that we look forward to experiencing after we breathe our last. It is not synonymous with "heaven" or "afterlife." Eternal life is what we experience from the womb to the tomb and beyond. As Christians, we believe that death marks not an end, but a transition from one stage of eternal life to another, from the Church Militant to the Church Triumphant. To us, the faithful departed are dead, but they are not dead and gone. In the words of a majestic prayer, they "rejoice with us, but upon another shore and in a greater light."[2]

Funerals are about hope. First, admittedly, we focus on hope for the deceased. As the body is carried into the church, we proclaim, recalling Jesus' words to Martha: "I am the Resurrection and the life." And then, even as the gaze of the mourners is fixed on a

1. Episcopal Church, "Commemoration of the Dead," 382.
2. Episcopal Church, "Bidding Prayer."

casket or an urn containing the earthly remains of their loved one, we continue in the words of Jesus' own declaration of hope: "He that believeth in me, though he were dead, yet shall he live, and whosoever believeth in me shall never die" (John 11:25).

Hymnody complements liturgy, as we sing hope-filled verses written throughout two millennia of Christian witness. They describe the hope of eternal bliss of the saints in light ("Oh what their joy and their glory must be/Those endless sabbaths the blessed ones see"). They describe the hope of the heavenly city where the departed have, as it were, taken up residence ("Jerusalem the golden with milk and honey blest"). They describe the hope of new relationships with each other, ("where knitting severed friendships us and partings are no more") and the hope of new relationships with God in the joy of the Resurrection through Jesus Christ ("He walks with me and he talks with me along the narrow way").[3]

But while music can do much to enhance the beauty of funerals, and the liturgy itself can offer a dignified and Spirit-filled framework befitting so solemn an occasion, most would agree that it is the sermon that is the linchpin of the funeral. Friends seeking a report of a funeral service they missed are unlikely to ask the name of the song rendered by the soloist and are even less likely to ask which rite was used. But almost invariably they will want to know something about what the preacher had to say. What was her message? Did she bring comfort to the family in their hour of need? Did she know Aunt Hattie?—which is not interpreted as "Were they bosom buddies?" but rather, did she understand Aunt Hattie and appreciate her place in the church, the family, and her community? Was there a personal, reassuring word from the pulpit, or was the preacher's style distant and aloof?

If funerals are about hope, the funeral sermon must not concentrate exclusively on hope for the deceased but must also concern itself—to an even greater extent—with the hope of the mourners. Few worshippers believe that the funeral service

3. Hymn references are, respectively, to Abelard, "O What Their Joy;" Neale, "Jerusalem the Golden;" Alford, "Ten-Thousand Times Ten-Thousand;" and Ackley, "I Serve a Risen Savior."

actually effects the transition of the dead person from this world to the next; most, indeed, express a belief that Aunt Hattie is already, through the grace of God, "in God's hands" or "in a better place." Above all, the sermon is a message of hope for the bereaved. As one writer poignantly observes: "When somebody dies . . . there is only that moment in which to speak the Gospel to the sharp, fresh pain of the survivors. It is necessary to write a word of hope in the concrete of their experience before it hardens."[4] Every person attending a funeral is reminded of his own mortality. The service causes that person to contemplate how the rest of his life should be spent, and the preacher must be able to seize on that kairotic moment when the bereaved might be able to be inspired by the life of the deceased and may even be contemplating amendment of life.

How is this to be accomplished? If the funeral sermon is to offer to the bereaved a glimpse of that "sure and certain hope" in the Resurrection, it can do so by demonstrating how in her life, her earthly pilgrimage, Aunt Hattie strove to live into the joy of the Resurrection; how she, however imperfect, was a vessel of God's grace. Whether a close family relation or a person who is not a member of any faith community but has come simply to pay respects—for it must be remembered that funeral preaching presents a unique evangelistic opportunity—the person who worships at a funeral service wants to learn from Aunt Hattie's example and be able to sing with her, "For the saints of God are just folk like me/ And I mean to be one too."[5]

There is a problem, however, in such an approach to funeral preaching—of which I am acutely aware, having relied on such an approach myself—namely, that in using "material" from the life of the deceased, the homilist runs the risk of delivering a eulogy and not a sermon. Inspired, perhaps, by Marc Antony, who prefaced his funeral sermon for Julius Caesar by stating "I come to bury Caesar, not to praise him," many preachers have admonished their

4. Hoffacker, *Matter of Life and Death*, 7.
5. Scott, "I Sing a Song of the Saints of God," 293.

colleagues to eschew any expression of praise for the deceased, and stick to the Gospel instead![6]

But whereas Antony justifies his approach by contending that "the evil that men do lives after them; the good is oft interred with their bones," many funeral preachers,when plying their trade, seem pleased to inter, in the same osseous mix, good deeds along with the bad, by delivering generic homilies on the Resurrection, (a practice described by one pastor as "to whom it may concern" sermons) with nary a word about how the deceased shares in that Resurrection.[7] Such a practice is especially lamentable, since the preacher should be aware that, unlike a Sunday congregation, the worshippers at a funeral are united in a common purpose, namely, to give thanks for the life of a departed loved one.

Some reasons given for omitting laudatory references to the departed stem from the fear that any attempt to praise the dead might come across as depriving God of God's due, since all worship, as most theologians understand it, is presumed to exist first and foremost for the praise of the Almighty.[8] One pastor asserts that the funeral sermon is "preaching from the Scripture," and therefore allows personal data about the deceased to be expressed by a family member or friend only after the sermon is delivered or before the service begins.[9] There is also what can be described as the "egalitarian approach," which contends that nothing should be done to make a difference between people at the time of death. Still others have opined that any praise of the deceased runs the risk of being disingenuous. The late dean of the American Cathedral in

6. Directions for funerals in the Roman Catholic Church, for example, state: "A brief homily based on the readings is always given after the Gospel reading and may also be given after the readings at the vigil service; but there is never to be a eulogy". (Catholic Church, *Order of Christian Funerals*, 8.)

7. Hughes, *Trumpet in Darkness*, 10.

8. See, for example, Willimon, *Worship as Pastoral Care*, 115: "Against the definition of the purpose of a funeral as being 'for the family,' I argue that the purpose is the same as for any service of Christian worship: to worship God."

9. Schmitz, *Life of Christ*, 16.

Paris famously quipped: "Eulogies are difficult. It is wrong to have one person lying in the nave and another lying in the pulpit."[10]

Much of the criticism of eulogies is valid. Eulogies do have as their subject matter a life that is past as opposed to a future consummation of that life in the divine presence. They do emphasize human accomplishments as opposed to what God has wrought through the agency of women and men. But I am not suggesting that funeral preachers should mount the pulpit and present a eulogy as if it were a citation for Aunt Hattie's candidacy for an honorary degree, but instead to present vignettes from an earthly pilgrimage that make her worthy for enrollment in the Book of Life.

The funeral sermon is not a eulogy. It is, rather, a scriptural message illustrated by eulogistic examples. The sermons in this book are replete with such examples. Sue Boulden's passion for social justice, for instance, is nothing less than her living out the spirit of the Beatitudes. The reference to Attorney Charles Arensberg's volunteer work in the Mississippi Delta at the height of the Civil Rights Movement is not an item randomly plucked from his resume; it is, rather, a description of his self-sacrifice on behalf of the least, the lost, and the last of this society, and a commitment, on his part, to follow our Lord's example to serve and not to be served. Examples of how Ardelle Hopson saw virtually every aspect of the Christian faith through the lens of stewardship are meant to convey to the congregation the extent to which she believed in sharing time, talent, and treasure for the building up of Christ's Kingdom. The stories about Bishop Martin's contention against racial injustice are emblematic of his lifelong struggle to encourage the people of God to respect the dignity of every human being, as promised in the Baptismal Covenant.

The twenty-six homiletic offerings that follow fall into three categories. In "Mentors," I share sermons that I preached at the funerals of five clergymen, all of whom had a profound effect on me at various stages of my ministerial formation. "Matriarchs" is made up of homilies delivered at obsequies for women of deep

10. Leo, *Exits and Entrances*, 16.

faith and devotion, "pillars" of Calvary Episcopal Church, Pittsburgh, who distinguished themselves as leaders in their families, their parish, and the broader community. "All sorts and conditions of men" is an expression borrowed from The Book of Common Prayer.[11] Originally, the phrase sufficed as a reference to all people, but I have chosen here to use it in its literal sense, as these sermons were delivered at the funerals of men who represented a broad spectrum of humankind and who impacted those around them in myriad ways—among them a young man who committed suicide, a newspaper editor, a diplomat, a priest, a football player, a violinist, an industrialist, and a university chancellor. These and others whose funeral sermons I have been privileged to preach, represent people of God who manifested "the varieties of gifts but the same Spirit" of which St Paul speaks (1 Cor 12:4), whom we commend to God's care in sure and certain hope of the Resurrection to eternal life.

In the compilation of this volume, I am indebted for technical support to Ken Smith, director of communications at Calvary Church, Marsha Morris, parish secretary, and to my son, Justin Lewis; and to my friend and colleague Richard Burnett for his gracious and insightful Foreword.

Harold T. Lewis
Pittsburgh:
The Feast of St. Mark, Apostle & Evangelist
25 April 2018

11. "Prayer for All Conditions of Men," 32.

I. MENTORS

"God doesn't choose the worthy."

PERCIVAL ALAN REX McFARLANE, Priest (1928–2001)
Preached in St. Mary's Church, Paddington, London
2 February 2001

> I am the Good Shepherd. The Good Shepherd lays down
> his life for the sheep. (John 10:11)

ALMOST EXACTLY FORTY YEARS ago, I found myself in the role
of president of what we used to call the YPF—the Young People's
Fellowship—in St. Philip's Church, Brooklyn, New York, where
I had grown up. Between masses, the youth of the parish served
breakfast to the faithful and charged the princely sum of a dol-
lar and twenty-five cents. Now the only people who didn't pay
for breakfast were the reverend clergy of the parish, an awesome
threesome, who arrived, at the stroke of ten, in cassocks and biret-
tas. It was on such a Sunday breakfast that one of those priests
approached me and, out of the blue, asked me what I wanted to
do with my life. I told him I wanted to become an interpreter at
the United Nations. Without batting an eyelash, he asked me if I
had ever considered the priesthood. I laughed so loud that people
stopped eating their breakfast. When I regained some of my com-
posure, I said, "Oh no, Father, I am not cut out for for that sort of
thing." The priest's retort—he was deadly serious—made me stop
laughing. "Harold," he said, "God does not choose the worthy, he
makes worthy those whom he chooses." "Not a bad line," I thought
to myself, and I promised the priest that I would, like Mary, ponder

3

these things in my heart. That priest was, of course, Percival Alan Rex McFarlane, beloved curate at St. Philip's and known to young and old alike as "Father Mac."

Father Mac took charge of my life. He told me to apply to McGill University, and, when I was admitted, he arranged for me to stay at the Diocesan Theological College and to worship at his boyhood parish, the Church of St. John the Evangelist. When, a year or two later, he returned to Montreal, ostensibly to work as chaplain at Her Majesty's Prison (but really, I suspect, to keep an eye on me) he informed me that, for my soul's health, I should come to to prison to play the organ for the Sunday services—for free, of course. He was always giving me life lessons. Once, he visited me at college and brought with him a young man who had been formerly an inmate. Alan spent fifteen minutes on the telephone explaining that it would be unethical to let on that I had met this man when he was behind bars while I was the prison chapel organist. He had, after all, paid his debt to society. I assured Alan that I understood. Over sherry, one of my classmates asked Alan's guest how he came to know Father McFarlane The former prisoner, doubtless also schooled by Alan, replied, "I met him on the outside."

Today, as we gather to commend Alan to Jesus Christ, the Bishop and Shepherd of our souls, in whose priesthood Alan was pleased to share, we take no small comfort in Jesus' words in the tenth chapter of Saint John's Gospel: "I am the good shepherd: the good shepherd lays down his life for the sheep. He who is an hireling and not a shepherd sees the wolf coming and leaves the sheep and flees; and the wolf snatches them and scatters them . . . I am the good shepherd; I know my own and my own know me, as the Father, and I lay down my life for the sheep" (John 10:11–14).

I think this passage is especially appropriate for two reasons. First, Alan was a man who could mouth these words with conviction. Fully aware of his humanness, he could and did put himself in God's hands, in the embrace of a loving shepherd. He tried to tell me this in our last conversation on the telephone. "Your old Uncle Alan is dying," he said, in that knowing tone of voice that only the dying possess. And, in a brief moment, all my pastoral training went out the window, and I assumed the role of one who loved him and couldn't bear to let him go. Instead of helping Alan to prepare for a holy death (not that he needed my help, mind you!), I took the coward's way out; I was in denial. I knew I would be returning to London on February 19th and I assured him that we would see each other then. Alan was comforted by Jesus' assuring words, and could, therefore, commend his own soul to God: "I am the good shepherd; I know my own and my own know me."

But there is another reason that this passage is appropriate. And that is that Alan, as priest and pastor, emulated the Good Shepherd. When all was said and done, Alan would do anything for his friends. It was contrary to his nature to be like the hireling, the paid help who is indifferent to the plight of the sheep, who would run away and leave them to the wolves. Alan had that rare gift of being able to know many people intimately. And he knew us, our "downsittings and our uprisings," our foibles and our idiosyncrasies, and loved us for them, as we loved him.

We all have our Alan stories. We have been his friends, his confidants, his protégés, his companions, his nurses. At times, we have found him irascible and overbearing, even cantankerous and demanding. Yet through it all, his rapier wit kept us on our toes, his infectious laugh and his radiant smile bespoke his gentleness. When all is said and done, Alan was a loving, caring, human being who touched all of us. He was usually almost all too willing to push the envelope. Bishop Herbert Thompson of Southern Ohio wishes he could have been here today, and he sends he assurance of his prayers to Alan's family and friends. He, too, is indebted to Alan for having nudged him into the priesthood. One of Alan's favorite stories about Herb is that before Herb embraced Anglicanism, he was a Methodist. And while still a Methodist, Alan dressed him up in alb, tunicle, maniple, and biretta and put him through the paces of being subdeacon at Midnight Mass on Christmas Eve. Alan took pride in pointing out that the same dyed-in-the-wool Anglicans who were aghast that a mere Methodist would be allowed to be so gloriously arrayed are now dying for the privilege of touching the hem of now Bishop Thompson's episcopal garments!

So we gather today not so much to mourn Alan's loss, but to give thanks to Almighty God for his life and the lives of those who he has touched. We give thanks that Alan's life and witness have made a difference and that many of us are richer for having known him. We are tempted—although the span of Alan's life managed to equal that of the Psalmist's threescore years and ten—to say that he was snatched from us prematurely. But that's our personal agenda. Less selfish reflection enables us to say to Alan, as the Good Shepherd has said to him, "Well done, good and faithful servant. Enter into the joy of the Lord."

Let us pray:

> O what their joy and their glory must be,
> Those endless Sabbaths the blessed ones see:
> Crown for the valiant, to weary ones rest:
> God shall be all, and in all ever blest. AMEN.

"Do you have anything to declare?"

RICHARD BEAMON MARTIN, Bishop (1913–2012)
Preached in St. Philip's Church, Brooklyn
15 April 2012

> Having been disciplined a little, they will receive great
> good, because God tested them and found them worthy
> of himself. (Wis 3:4)

ABOUT FIFTY YEARS AGO, as an acolyte, serving at the altar of this
great parish, I sat in the sanctuary, vested in a starched cotta and a
black cassock. The palms of my hands were flat on my lap (one of
the strict rules of the acolyte warden, Mr. Butler) and I sat mesmer-
ized by the words emanating from this very pulpit. The preacher
was Father Martin, St. Philip's third rector, and he preached a sermon on the roads in the New Testament. The journey along each
of these roads—to Bethlehem, Damascus, Jerusalem, Calvary and
Emmaus—according to the preacher, had special significance for
the Christian life. Fast-forward twenty-five years. I found myself
sitting in the chancel of St. John's Church on the island of St. Croix,
resting my vocal chords after having sung the litany at the consecration of E. Don Taylor. Bishop Martin was holding forth from
the pulpit on the other side of the chancel. I found myself saying,
"My goodness, he sounds just like me," then quickly realized I had
put the cart before the horse. It was I who sounded like him. At
that moment, it became clear to me just how much that holy man
of God had served as a role model and mentor.

Nearly sixteen years ago, Bishop Martin graced the pulpit of Calvary Church, Pittsburgh, on the occasion of my institution as fifteenth rector. He started off his forty-five-minute sermon (delivered without the benefit of so much as a three by five index card) by saying that white parishes had been known to call black rectors before, but normally that happens when the senior warden looks to the church's ceiling and sees the sky, and when all kinds of sounds emanate from the organ when there is no one near the console! But this evening, I want to share with you, verbatim, the last sermon I ever heard Bishop Martin preach. His pulpit was a bed in the intensive care unit of Interfaith Hospital; no alb or rochet and chimere draped his frail frame, no brocade stole hung about his neck—a flimsy patient's gown, precariously tied at the neck and the waist, was the only vestment he wore, and then he preached a sermon in answer to my query about how he was feeling. "Harold," he proclaimed, "I am ninety-nine years old, blind, and I am marching on the King's Highway. Please give me your blessing." At that moment I felt like Timothy listening to Paul's valedictory: "I have fought the good fight, I have finished the course, I have kept the faith" (2 Tim 4:7). In dying, my friends, Bishop Martin taught us how to live.

My sisters and brothers in Christ, we have come together tonight to give thanks to Almighty God for the life and witness of Richard Beamon Martin, bishop in the church of God, master of the homiletic art, consummate pastor, and Christian gentleman. We commend to the never-failing providence of Almighty God a faithful servant who lived into his one hundredth year and whose ordained ministry spanned seven decades. I would like to suggest that King Solomon had Bishop Richard in mind when he wrote the words: "Having been disciplined a little, they will receive great good, because God tested them and found them worthy of himself" (Wis 3:5). Richard Martin lived his long life because he possessed, by the grace of God, an inner fortitude. It is precisely because he had been tested, precisely because he had borne the burden in the heat of the day, that he was able, at life's end, to appear before his

Maker in full possession of his intellect. Bishop Martin had lost the use of his eyes, but he was hardly blind.

Richard Martin was able to see through the folly of the commonly held misconception that everything in the church was just fine until the ordination of a gay bishop. The grandson of slaves, who worked as a yard boy for a white family and to whom cotton-picking was an everyday occurrence, he knew firsthand that, during the reportedly "good ol' days," there took place the historical disenfranchisement of a people who, in this country and this church, have been called successively Africans, coloreds, Negroes, Afro-Americans, and African Americans. Bishop Martin was instructed in the faith in a tiny, one-room chapel in Pawleys Island, South Carolina, while whites worshipped their Lord on several acres of prime land a few miles away. He remembered being told by his bishop that attending the Philadelphia Divinity School was not an option, because colored men who trained north of the Mason-Dixon Line had trouble adjusting to life in the South when they returned (read "they didn't stay in their place"). So like scores of men of his vintage, he attended the all-black Bishop Payne Divinity School. He also suffered the indignity of attending colored convocations at a time when blacks in Southern dioceses were not allowed to participate in diocesan conventions. And long before assuming the role of Archdeacon of Brooklyn, he was Archdeacon of Colored Work in the Diocese of Southern Virginia.

Even as a bishop, he learned that a black face often trumped a purple shirt, as when he was told by a rector whose congregation was expecting a white bishop that allowing Bishop Martin to officiate would be like offering hamburger to his flock when they were expecting sirloin—or when, upon his election and consecration, the not-so-subtle message was conveyed to Bishop and Mrs. Martin that taking up residence in the see city of his diocese would be problematic.

But let it be said that these and a host of other incidents never caused Bishop Martin's faith to flag. Racism never consumed him, never embittered him, and never deterred him from his mission and ministry. A clue to the reason for this is found in his book, *On the Wings of the Morning:* "Suffering," he wrote, "is distilled love that reveals the true nature of the spiritual stamina and foundation of the soul. Our part is to live with the questions; to live into the questions, to live beyond the questions." Such a view is part and parcel of his theology of ministry: "The essence of priesthood," believed Bishop Martin, "is reconciliation. It is by the grace of God that the priest stands as a sign and symbol of the reconciling Lord."[1]

Richard Martin was sometimes asked why he and other black people remained in the Episcopal Church. He answered that he believed "the black presence in the Episcopal Church is like yeast permeating the body politic to rise above exclusiveness to an acceptance of the reality that we are all God's children, one family under God." He believed, too, that black people offer their ability to joyfully overcome injustice and suffering.

Moreover, Richard Martin could find humor in the most painful experiences. My favorite story, which he always told with a chuckle, was about one of his first parish visitations, shortly after his consecration, in 1967. The church member assigned to meet the bishop's car and escort him and Mrs. Martin into the church waved frantically as the bishop approached, saying, "This spot is for Bishop Martin." When the bishop said that he was indeed Bishop Martin, the parishioner responded, "Excuse me, Bishop, but all the bishops of Long Island drive Cadillacs" (the bishop had arrived in an old Chevy). When Bishop Martin told the story to Bishop Sherman the next morning, the fifth bishop of Long Island picked up the telephone, called the Cadillac dealer, and ordered that a Cadillac be delivered to Bishop Martin. Hanging up the receiver, Bishop Sherman announced, "They won't have that excuse again."

When Bishop Walker telephoned me to inform me of Bishop Martin's death, he said, "This is the end of an era." And so it is. He was of the old school, in the best sense of that word. That means you could cut your finger on the crease in his pants and see your reflection in his shoes. That means that he was a catholic churchman who took seriously the fact that he was ordained to

1. Martin, *Wings of the Morning*, 39.

administer both word and sacrament; and took seriously the fact that the church of Jesus Christ, as Archbishop Temple reminded us, is the only organization that exists primarily for the benefit of those not its members. But he was not the kind of priest who could tell you how many times you should kiss the altar during the mass (seven, for the record) but found it difficult to offer an extemporaneous prayer of condolence or encouragement. When I entered the parish ministry forty years ago, Bishop Martin reminded me of the importance of being a pastor: "You can make the parish machinery hum, double the budget, and build new buildings, but unless you are there when your people need you, everything else you do is for naught."

Richard Beamon Martin was the oldest living bishop in the Episcopal Church. He witnessed sea changes in the life of the Episcopal Church and lived through the upheavals caused by women's ordination, Prayer Book revision, the civil rights movement, and, more recently, the debate over human sexuality. He was a deputy to the 1955 General Convention that took place in Honolulu because Tollie Caution and Thurgood Marshall stormed the Presiding Bishop's office demanding that the Convention not be held in Houston—where the bishop of Texas could not guarantee that housing could be provided for Negro deputies.

So what more can be said about a pastor, priest, and prophet who did so much in recent years, even after his so-called retirement, to keep the church on an even keel as she navigated uncharted waters, providing nurture and guidance, even from his bed of affliction, to his fellow bishops and to yet another generation of clergy?

The simple answer is we can say nothing at all. We who are dwarfed by his spiritual stature, humbled by his holy demeanor, and pauperized by the wealth of his experience and intellect can add not a jot or tittle to the legacy that Bishop Martin has bequeathed to us. What we can do, however, is imagine the words that were exchanged between him and the blessed Apostle Peter on the occasion of Bishop Martin's interview for admission to the Pearly Gates (one of Peter's easier jobs). The form of Saint Peter's question is identical to the question that customs agents ask at the airport:

Richard, bishop of the Church of God, do you have anything to declare? Bishop Martin responded "I declare that, like Jeremiah, the Lord God knew me before he formed me in my mother's womb, and sanctified me, and made me a prophet unto the nations."

Richard, bishop of the Church of God, do you have anything to declare? "I declare that I have endeavored, day by day, to be faithful to my vows as a deacon, to be modest and humble, and to have a ready will to observe all spiritual discipline."

Richard, bishop of the Church of God, do you have anything to declare? "I declare that I have endeavored, day by day, to be faithful to my vows as a priest, that I never cease in my labor until I have done all that lieth in me, to bring all such as are or shall be committed to my charge, unto that agreement in the faith and knowledge of God, and that there be no place left in me, either for error in religion or for viciousness in life."

Richard, bishop of the Church of God, do you have anything to declare? "I declare that I have endeavored, day by day, to be faithful to my vows as a husband, and did plight my troth to my beloved Annelle, for better for worse, for richer for poorer, in sickness and in health, till death us do part."

Richard, bishop of the Church of God, do you have anything to declare? "I declare that I have endeavored, day by day, to be faithful to my vows as a bishop, remembering to "stir up the grace of God, . . . for God hath not given us the spirit of fear, but of power, and love, and soberness."

Richard, bishop of the Church of God, do you have anything to declare? "I declare that I have endeavored, day by day, to be a source of and a force for reconciliation, bringing together all sorts and conditions of men and women, so that together we can sing:

> I'm gonna sit at the welcome table,
> I'm gonna sit at the welcome table,
> I'm gonna sit at the welcome table,
> One of these days.

Richard, bishop of the Church of God, do you have anything to declare? "I declare, in the words of the great priest and hymn-writer Charles Wesley,

> A charge to keep I have,
> A name to glorify,
> A never-dying soul to save,
> And fit it for the sky.
>
> To serve the present age,
> My calling to fulfill:
> O may it all my powers engage
> To do my master's will.
>
> Arm me with jealous care,
> As in Thy sight to live;
> And O Thy servant, Lord prepare
> A strict account to give!
>
> AMEN.

Ecclesiastical Polity Redux[2]

RICHARD HOOKER WILMER Jr., Priest (1918–2005)
Preached in Calvary Church, Pittsburgh
9 April 2005

> The Spirit of the Lord is upon me, because the Lord has anointed me. (Isa 61:1)

RICHARD WILMER WAS LARGER than life. This was true both literally and figuratively. I learned this thirty-seven years ago when, as a twenty-one-year-old seminarian who had just entered the Berkeley Divinity School, I met Dean Wilmer for the first time. I was young, idealistic, and probably just a tad rebellious, and fully believed that if only I could get a collar around my neck, I could save the world. And if Dick Wilmer was bemused by my youthful enthusiasm, he didn't let on. These were the Sixties, after all, when everybody wanted to save the world, and he knew, in his avuncular wisdom, that time, prayer, and three years at seminary would smooth out the rough edges. In some people, size, stature, and erudition can be threatening and overwhelming. Not so with Richard Wilmer. Those attributes in him, instead, commanded

---

2. Dr. Wilmer—and at least three of his ancestors—were named for Richard Hooker (1554–1600), whose writings, especially *Laws of Ecclesiastical Polity*, argued that Anglicanism can be understood in light of its foundation in Scripture, tradition, and reason (the so-called "three-legged stool"), and that, moreover, its genius is that it is the *via media*, a "middle way" that bridges catholic and protestant traditions. This spirit is manifest, indeed revived, in his ministry and that of his nineteenth-century forebears. See Hooker, *Laws*.

respect and admiration, and I have respected and admired him from those early years of my priestly formation until these most recent years, when I have had the privilege to be his pastor. The days on which I would bring him holy communion at Canterbury Place were special. After the service, we would sit for an hour or so and talk about the latest developments in the life of the church, and Dick not infrequently expressed his dismay over them. But his remarks were not empty laments; they were the theologically insightful and often analytical comments one would expect from an Oxford-trained historian. Neither of us could know when we met nearly four decades ago that I would one day have the honor to preach his funeral, and it is an honor that I shall always cherish.

To understand Richard Hooker Wilmer Jr., his life and his legacy, we have to go back to the middle of the sixteenth century, to the birth of Richard Hooker. Hooker was a priest and theologian who did more than anyone, before or since, to explain the way Anglicans think, pray, and act—and Lord knows, we could use him today! But Hooker did more than steer a middle way between catholic excesses and puritan deficiencies. He believed that the church is primarily an agent of reformation, the means by which we realize our full potential. To Hooker, the church exists for the benefit of humankind, and when it fails to function in this capacity, it falls short of its mission. Hooker, in short, laid a foundation for Anglican social witness.

Why do I drag a history lesson into this funeral sermon? Because I don't think it was coincidental that two hundred years after the birth of this great theologian, the great-grandfather of our brother departed was baptized Richard Hooker. His parents obviously had great things in store for him, and they proved to be prophetic. The first Richard Hooker Wilmer became the bishop of Alabama, and one of his most enduring legacies is that, in 1883, when all the bishops of the Southern dioceses met at Sewanee and voted to disenfranchise all black Episcopalians, placing them under the paternalistic control of a white bishop, Richard Hooker Wilmer's was the sole dissenting vote. That mountaintop in Tennessee was to prove a significant locale for the Wilmers because,

exactly seventy years later, when the University of the South refused to open its doors to black students, Richard Wilmer Jr., the
University chaplain, joined the faculty of the University's School of
Theology and resigned their positions, and left en masse. Wilmers
have obviously believed that unless you stand for something, you
will fall for anything. They have not been afraid to stand up, even
in the face of prevailing contrary opinion, and uphold a righteous
cause. Not all Wilmers have been priests, alas, but in each generation, be they celebrated physicians or renowned attorneys, they
have distinguished themselves in their dedication to their fellow
human beings. But while the world will remember Dick Wilmer
as a renowned historian and even a social activist, his family will
remember him as a loving paterfamilias. His five children and ten
grandchildren will always hold him as that doting, solicitous man
who was devoted to them and who, while in good health, spent
his time showing up for all their rites of passage. To Sarah, Dick
will forever be the man who, though suffering from Alzheimer's,
always brightened when she came into the room. "Who am I?" she
would quiz him. And without fail, the answer would come, "You
are my beautiful bride, Sarah." Some enterprising soul, by the way,
should go to Hollywood and make a film about their life. It could
be called "Dick and Sarah—the Movie." The real-life story has
drama, intrigue, humor, pathos, and unexpected twists in the plot.
The movie would start off, of course, making it abundantly clear to
the audience that yes, Sarah married Dick for his money—seven-
ty-five cents, to be exact. Their first encounter was in an airport.
Bad weather had caused their Atlanta-bound flight to be diverted,
and, in this pre-cell phone age, everyone was queuing up at the
pay phones—remember them? Sarah ran out of change and a rude
operator was threatening to terminate her call, so she turned in
desperation to the handsome gentleman behind her in the line,
and asked, "Sir, could you possibly lend me some quarters?" The
rest is history.

Given Dick Wilmer's life of service, it is no surprise that he
chose for the Old Testament lesson today the very verses from
Isaiah that Jesus used as the text for his first sermon in the temple

at Nazareth: "The Lord has anointed me . . . to bind up the broken-hearted, to proclaim liberty to the captives and release to those in prison, to proclaim a year of the Lord's favor" (Isa 61:1). Whether as professor or priest, husband or grandfather, Dick was selfless. His life showed forth as a combination of noblesse oblige and servant ministry, humility and compassion. But I think Dick chose this lesson, too, for it contains a message for those whom he leaves behind. "Comfort all who mourn, give them garlands instead of ashes, oil of gladness instead of mourners' tears" (Isa 61:3). Today we do not so much lament his death as we give thanks for his life, a life we can honor by taking a page from his book, by seeing him and holding him up as a shining example of how to lead a godly, righteous, and sober life. AMEN.

"Wear your life like a loose garment."

FRANKLIN DELTON TURNER, Bishop (1933–2013)
Preached in Philadelphia Episcopal Cathedral
11 January 2014

Let not your hearts be troubled. (John 14:1)

I FIRST MET FRANK Turner forty years ago, at the General Convention in Louisville. I was looking for a job, and Frank was about to have draped over his shoulders Tollie Caution's venerable mantle as "Deputy for Colored Work," or, as it had been restyled, Staff Officer for Black Ministries. Frank and I had countless conversations over the years, but two stand out. The first was a talk we had as I was about to succeed him at 815, in which he gave me some advice which, admittedly, I seldom heeded: "Harold," he said, "you don't always have to have an opinion." The second was a conversation we had on one of the occasions that Frank was running for bishop. It took place during the period of limbo between the walkabouts (the dignified name we have given to what used to be known in the trade as the "dog and pony show") and the election itself. I pummeled Frank with a barrage of questions: How did it go? Were there any surprise questions? What do you think your chances are? Do you think the people in that diocese are ready for a black bishop? As the conversation—more like an inquisition—ensued, it became painfully obvious that I was far more anxious about the election than Frank was. When I finally came up for air and gave Frank an opportunity to respond, he simply said, "Harold, I am wearing the election like a loose garment."

My sisters and brothers in Christ, as we gather today in this cathedral church to commend our brother Franklin Delton Turner, bishop in the church of God, to the never-failing care of Jesus, the Bishop and Shepherd of our souls, I would like to suggest to you that in those few words Frank succinctly expressed his philosophy, his theology, his approach to life.

Frank wore life like a loose garment. He was unflappable, a calm presence. He knew who he was and Whose he was. It was Frank whom Rudyard Kipling had in mind when he wrote the poem, "If":

> If you can keep your head when all about you
>
> Are losing theirs and blaming it on you,
>
> If you can trust yourself when all men doubt you,
>
> But make allowance for their doubting too.[3]

Frank exuded a self-confidence that was always tinged with humility and not arrogance. He was the sixth of seven children born to a maid and a sharecropper in rural North Carolina during the Great Depression, yet he told me it wasn't until he was sitting in a freshman sociology class at Livingstone College that he learned that he was poor. This, as he explained to me, was because of the sense of pride and self-worth instilled in him by his family and his teachers. Neither his humble roots nor his race were seen by Frank as detriments to life and ministry; in fact, they were understood to be gifts which could be offered to the broader community. Thus, Frank could say with Saint Paul: "I know what it is to be in need, and I know what it is to have plenty. I have learned the secret of being content in any and every situation, whether well fed or hungry, whether living in plenty or in want" (Phil 4:12).

That ability to function "in any and every situation" was put to the test early. Frank was nurtured in the faith in the AME Zion Church, but when he became disillusioned with that church, owing to concerns both theological and political, he remembered

3. Kipling, "If," 170.

the kindness of Fr. Tom Blair, rector of St. Luke's, Salisbury, who served as de facto Episcopal chaplain to Livingstone and once had told Frank that the Episcopal Church needed "good colored clergy." He gladly received Frank and dispatched him to an interview with the bishop coadjutor. Bishop Baker asked Frank some well-chosen questions, the most poignant of which was, "What do you think about the integration of our schools?" It was about 1957, and Brown vs. Board of Education had been met with mixed reviews in the South. The future bishop suffragan of Pennsylvania responded in a way that indicated he already had a firm grasp of the principle of Anglican compromise: "Integration must go forward," he answered, "but it might be best to move gradually, to ensure that it is properly implemented." The bishop liked the answer so much that he invoked its theme in his next convention address. Frank, meanwhile, moved through the ranks "with all deliberate speed." On three successive days, not long after his interview, he was confirmed, accepted as a postulant for holy orders, and licensed as a lay reader—progress unheard of since the election and ordination of Saint Ambrose!

Today's Gospel lesson contains these words: "Let not your hearts be troubled"—and, with all due respect to any New Testament scholars who may be in the congregation, I think (pun intended) a loose translation of our Lord's words could well be, "Wear your life like a loose garment." You see, Jesus uses these words as he speaks to his disciples in a moment of crisis. Gathered together in the Upper Room, he tells them that he will be departing from them, but he admonishes them, "Let not your hearts be troubled." The disciples didn't know or understand where he would be going, and it was not at all certain if they could go with him. But Jesus tells them nevertheless, "Let not your hearts be troubled." Jesus himself had cause for concern; he knew that one of his disciples would be a traitor, and that even Peter, his chief lieutenant, would deny he even knew his Lord. Yet Jesus insists on encouraging them with the words, "Let not your hearts be troubled."

Everything seemed to be on the verge of collapse, but Jesus told them not to worry, not to fear, not to fret. Jesus was warning them of the type of fear that leads to paralysis, when we worry so much (often in the time of crisis), we become so depressed, that we are unable to function. Worry, as someone once said, is like rocking in a rocking chair; it gives you something to do, but it doesn't get you anyplace.

If there were times during Frank Turner's ministry that his heart was troubled, we couldn't tell by his actions. He refused to fret. He refused to be overcome. During his senior year at seminary, recruiters from the National Church world mission department came to see if any of the soon-to-be graduates would be interested in serving in the mission field in Central and South America or perhaps Africa. Frank expressed an interest, only to be told, in the year of our Lord 1965, that the people—people of color—in the field would not accept a Negro as a pastor among them because they were accustomed to having white men in authority. Frank lengthened his loins and strengthened his stakes and accepted one of the two domestic colored missions that were offered to him.

For years, black Episcopalians have talked about the tensions between those whose roots are in the United States and those whose roots are in the West Indies. Are you more or less authentic if your ancestors harvested sugar cane instead of cotton? While most were content to talk about the situation and each other, trading in stereotypes and innuendos, Frank took action and convened a conference on the subject. With the wisdom of Isaiah, who said "Come let us reason together though are sins be like scarlet" (Isa 1:18), he called us together, initiated discussions and learned papers, and even arranged for them to be published in the St. Luke's Journal of Theology.

When Frank arrived at 815 in 1972, and surveyed the wreckage of the ill-fated General Convention Special Program, he didn't spend time weeping over the remains. Instead, he became a mediator and reconciler between disgruntled whites and disenfranchised blacks, and worked assiduously to encourage blacks to focus on building up their congregations through evangelism, communications, and Christian education.

Frank Turner could accomplish all these things because he always saw himself as "marching to Zion, beautiful, beautiful Zion." In a meditation on the theme "Zion," which formed part of a major address he delivered to the Union of Black Episcopalians in 1980, he said this:

> Zion touches an autobiographical nerve which moves me to remember how I got to where I am and, at the same time, helps me to see where I want to get to, when the sin-soiled, troubled clothes of this life will be shed; when these chilly waters of racial abuse and humiliation will no longer engulf me; when all of the valleys of despair will give way to ravines of true freedom and unending joy in the presence of the Lamb, King of Kings and Lord of Lords whom I shall see face to face.

With your indulgence, I would like to add one more word to this tribute to my dear friend. In the annals of ascetic theology, that branch of theology that deals with spirituality and self-discipline, there is a phrase which, unfortunately, we don't come across much any more. That phrase is "a holy death." A holy death is a departure from this life which is peaceful, sublime, and sanctified. It can even be a source of inspiration to those who witness it. The person who experiences a holy death is not anxious, wracked with fear, or concerned about whether he or she has set things right with family or with God. In a holy death, there is complete and utter confidence in God's mercy. In a holy death, there is no torment or angst. As a holy death approaches, the person who is dying can visualize the angels coming to bear his or her soul to Abraham's bosom. A holy death is, I think, what the Prayer Book tries to convey in the words of an intercession: "That we may end our lives in faith and hope, without suffering and without reproach." And the hymn on the lips of the person experiencing a holy death would doubtless be "Abide with me":

> I fear no foe, with thee at hand to bless:
> Ills have no weight, and tears no bitterness,
> Where is death's sting? Where, grave, thy victory?

I triumph still, if thou abide with me.[4]

It is my firm belief that Bishop Franklin Turner experienced a holy death. I had the privilege of sitting at his bedside just three days before he breathed his last. I became, in those precious hours, Frank's amanuensis—I was Timothy to his Paul, quill in hand, listening to and recording his final thoughts. And as he expressed those thoughts, he flashed a smile that could only be described as radiant. He told me that Barbara wanted to put a television in his room, but he vetoed that suggestion. TV would be a distraction, he said. He preferred to use the time left to him to think about what—and who—had been important in his life. He wanted to spend the time reminiscing about people whose lives he had touched. He wanted to reflect on how God had used him as a priest and a bishop, and if he had been faithful to his call. He said he wanted to ponder his raison d'être as a minister of the Gospel.

Frank wanted to give thanks for those stalwarts and role models in the faith, like Richard Martin, John Burgess, and John Allin, on whose shoulders he was privileged to stand. Moreover, he wanted to give thanks to all those folk, clergy and lay, who had ministered to him throughout his ministry and to him and his family over the past several months, who cooked, ran errands, and brought them communion. And, most of all, he wanted to thank God for his family: for Barbara, the love of his life, his soul mate, his partner in life and ministry for fifty years, and his children, Jennifer, Kim, and Petey. This, as even the casual observer could note, was a loving, close-knit family, and their home, in the words of the Prayer Book, was "a haven of blessing and of peace." And Frank beamed at the mention of his grandchildren, Kendell, Gabriel and Linez.

His family all reported that they were prepared, they were ready, and they were spiritually fortified for what lay ahead, precisely because Frank, in valiantly facing death, had given them hope—the sure and certain hope of resurrection to eternal life through our Lord Jesus Christ. As in every other phase of his

4. Lyte, "Abide With Me."

existence for fourscore years, Franklin Delton Turner had worn his impending death like a loose garment. In dying, Frank taught us how to live!

> Rest eternal grant unto Frank, O Lord, and let light perpetual shine upon him. May his soul, and the souls of all the faithful departed through the mercy of God, rest in peace and rise in glory. AMEN.

"God is working his purpose out as year succeeds to year."

WALTER CAMERON RIGHTER, Bishop (1923–2011)
Preached in Calvary Church, Pittsburgh
15 September 2011

Behold, I make all things new. (Rev 21:5)

IN THE YEAR OF grace 1951, six long decades ago, Harry Truman sat in the White House, color television made its debut, the Japanese peace treaty was signed in San Francisco, and J.D. Salinger published *Catcher in the Rye*. Meanwhile, in the Episcopal Church, it was business as usual. Henry Knox Sherrill, a scholar, patrician, and one of a long line of distinguished clerics, was presiding bishop. In the South, many black Episcopalians were barred from diocesan conventions and met in what were known as colored convocations. Women, the real backbone of the church, were mostly relegated to something called an auxiliary, and gays and lesbians were in the deepest recesses of the closet.

It was in that same year that Walter Cameron Righter, whose vocation was nurtured in a foxhole during the Battle of the Bulge and whose theological education was augmented by working in a Homestead steel mill during summer and holiday breaks from seminary, was ordained deacon and priest in the Diocese of Pittsburgh. He began his ministry, it can be said, making bricks without straw. Having already run a Sunday school at St. Stephen's, Sewickley and planted a congregation in Ligonier, he served a congregation in Aliquippa, which doubled because Walter made the radical decision to invite African Americans into its fellowship.

Two decades later, when Walter was consecrated seventh bishop of Iowa, the Episcopal Church, in the words of historiographer John Booty, had been "bolted out of its complacency." Women could be deacons and could even sit as deputies on the floor of General Convention! Presiding Bishop John Hines challenged the church to minister to the least, the lost, and the last of society; and the church, in an effort to catch up with the civil rights movement (and with Walter) began to demonstrate an interest in racial reconciliation.

Walter, who has been described as the "quintessential parish priest," a man with the heart of a pastor, a man committed to ministering to "all sorts and conditions" of people, was guided, I think, by words in the service of consecration—words not uttered at his own consecration since, by the time he became bishop, the church was using *Services for Trial Use.* (Some of us, of riper years, remember the "Zebra Book" and the "Green Book" and other interim manuals of worship that littered our pews!) Those words, which, unfortunately, bishops no longer hear, are these: "Remember that thou stir up the grace of God, which is given thee by this Imposition of our hands; for God hath not given us the spirit of fear, but of power, and love, and soberness."

Walter embraced the theology of the old Prayer Book, which would maintain that, although grace is a gift of God, an unmerited gift of God given to us mere mortals as the means through which we receive salvation, it is a gift that needs to be released, to be stirred up. Like the ingredients of a soup or a stew, it is not enough to put them in a pot and light the fire. No, the cook must stir, must blend those ingredients to bring out their full taste, their full potential. The cook and the bishop must be catalysts. But the bishop, like the cook, must be bold enough to carry out a grace-filled ministry enhanced, if you will, by new flavors. The bishop and the cook must be fearless.

The most powerful moment of consecration is the imposition of hands. The *Veni Creator Spiritus* having been sung, the consecrating bishops gather round the ordinand and lay their hands on his or her head, transmitting the sevenfold gifts of the Holy Spirit. At that moment, all those bishops are two thousand years old, engaged in the ancient and venerable rite through which the unbroken line of episcopal authority is transmitted. The concept of apostolic succession comes alive.

But there is, I am afraid, a standard joke about this picture in which the ordaining bishops seem to take an inordinate amount of time huddled round the ordinand, who disappears under the weight of twenty or more palms. It is said that, in too many cases, what is really happening is that the new bishop's spine is being removed!

In such cases, the bishop believes that the two tabs hanging from the mitre stand not for the two Testaments of Holy Scripture but for the two apostolic rites the bishop is ordained to perform—showing up and dressing up! Such a bishop has not heard the words, "God hath not given us the spirit of fear, but of power, and love, and soberness" (2 Tim 1:7). As a result, he or she is afraid to say anything that conveys a clear opinion, lest some offense be created thereby. Such a bishop, unduly influenced by the latest theology of mutual or shared ministry, is afraid to say anything not cleared by a committee, real or imagined. Such a bishop, as is often discovered too late, is rendered powerless and worse, in a very real sense, incapable of demonstrating love.

My sisters and brothers in Christ, we have come together today to commit to God's unfailing love and care the soul of Walter Cameron Righter, fearless bishop in the church of God. From what I have learned from Walter over this past decade that he has been in our midst, I know that he would not want us to unduly eulogize him, heaping homiletic flattery on his head to such an extent as to render him unrecognizable. No, Walter would want to be remembered not as an exemplary man, just a little lower than the angels, but rather as a faithful man, set apart for a ministry in Christ's holy catholic church. He would be the first to say that God doesn't choose the worthy, but makes worthy those whom He chooses.

His faithfulness might best be summed up in the words of today's lesson from the book of Revelation: "Behold I make all things new." It is not for naught that one of his favorite hymns, which we sang this morning, is "God is working his purpose out as year succeeds to year." Walter believed that the Christian faith is not static but dynamic, that revelation is an ongoing process, and that our salvation can never be pinpointed to a particular hour, day, or time, but is also an ongoing process. Walter would eschew the idea of "the faith once delivered to the saints" because the people who use that phrase are themselves uncertain as to which "once" is being referenced—Mt. Sinai, Caesarea Philippi, Nicaea, Chalcedon, or the Windsor Report.

In a famous sermon on the text, "Behold, I make all things new," Martin Luther King Jr. tells the story of Rip Van Winkle, who slept through the American Revolution. When he went to sleep, he could see in every public place a portrait of George III, but when he woke up twenty years later, he found that the king's picture had been replaced by a likeness of George Washington. Rip didn't get it! Dr. King warns us of the danger of sleeping through a revolution. He says: "All too many people find themselves living among a great period of social change, and they fail to develop the new attitudes, the new mental responses, that the new situation demands. They end up sleeping through a revolution."[5]

Bishop Righter was no Rip Van Winkle! While many around him slept or even suffered from self-induced comas during recent social revolutions, Walter was awake and vigilant, listening for a word from the Lord, and asking him for the grace to be faithful. His advocacy on behalf of racial minorities, women, and, most notably, for gays and lesbians came about as a process that involved re-examining previously held social and political prejudices; Walter could embrace new understandings because he was humble enough to ask God what God would have him do. And the answer always came back: "Do justice."

Walter was a loving husband and father. And today, Nancy, his children, and his grandchildren rise up and call him blessed.

5. King, "Remaining Awake," 206.

Walter was a priest and counted it a great privilege to offer up the Holy Eucharist, and, when denied that privilege by the ecclesiastical authority, I found that he was no less sacerdotal as he pontificated over a lunch table at Eat 'n Park, polishing off a dessert of lemon pie with at least two inches of meringue!

Walter was a prophet—not one who predicted the future, but one who, like Isaiah and Amos of old, interpreted the signs of the times for his people.

Walter was a pioneer, never afraid to break new ground, to chart a new path, and always willing, like his Lord, the Pioneer and Perfecter of the Faith, to make all things new. AMEN.

II. MATRIARCHS

Centenarian Sensibilities

HARRIET GRIER DONWORTH (1901–2003)
Preached in Calvary Church, Pittsburgh
22 April 2003

Martha said, "I believe that you are the Christ, the Son of
God." (John 11:27)

WHEN HARRIET GRIER WAS born in 1901, William McKinley was
in the White House and Queen Victoria was on the British throne.
Carrie Nation was running around wielding an axe and, on the
local scene, J. P. Morgan bought out Andrew Carnegie and formed
US Steel. Hattie shared her year of birth with such notables as Walt
Disney, Clark Gable, Emperor Hirohito, and Louis Armstrong, but
she outlived them all! Born during the Boer War, Hattie entered
Vassar College in the year that World War I broke out, was wid-
owed and remarried by the end of World War II, and breathed her
last as the United States was strategizing for what will probably be
remembered in history as the Second Gulf War. So we gather today
in Calvary Church (which, as her daughter Eleanor has reminded
us, Hattie watched being built) not so much to mourn the loss of
Harriet Grier Donworth, but to celebrate her long life, a life which
spanned all but eleven months of the twentieth century, and made
a foothold into the twenty-first.

Of all the bits of information that Mrs. Donworth shared with
me during my visits across the street to bring her communion,
what stands out most was her informing me that she had decided to

donate her body to science. It seemed, at first, a shocking wish for someone of her generation, but as I got to know her, I learned that that decision was consistent with two aspects of her personality: her philosophy and her theology. First, Hattie was nothing if she was not practical. She simply knew that her body would be of no use to her after death, but might well prove to prove to be of some value to gerontologists and others. It is not every day, after all, that medical types have the opportunity to gain insights from the body of a spry centenarian! But second, Hattie was unconventional—a free spirit. This, after all, was the woman who tooled around in a racy sports car at the age of twenty, and who could be seen, seventy years later, walking up Negley Hill, much to the astonishment of onlookers half her age.

Her practicality and unconventionality extended to matters liturgical as well. I had the privilege of reciting with Mrs. Donworth the confession, the canticles, and the versicles and responses from Morning Prayer, which she had committed to memory, a feat which stood her in good stead after her eyesight began to fail. Some years ago, she went through the Burial Office in her 1928 Prayer Book with a sharp pencil, and wrote either "Yes" or "No" in the margins next to prayers and lessons which she wanted to have read or did not want to have read at her funeral. We honor the spirit of those wishes and hope that Hattie will forgive us for using Rite I of the 1979 Prayer Book, which preserves the language and the cadence of her beloved 1928. Moreover, we trust that Hattie, now in those eternal habitations where timepieces are irrelevant, will grant us absolution for exceeding the ten-minute limit she placed on her obsequies!

This morning's Gospel tells the familiar story of Jesus' visit to his friends, Mary and Martha of Bethany, at the time when their brother, Lazarus, had just died. If we can imagine these two women as the Grier sisters, there is no doubt in our mind that Hattie's alter ego would be Martha. It was the feisty, somewhat confrontational, thinking-out-of-the-box Martha who takes Jesus on. She starts off with a complaint: "Lord, if you had been here, our brother would not have died." She said this because she knew that Jesus had a pipeline to his heavenly Father, and that whatever he wished would be given to him. And we can farther imagine Hattie doing some theological sparring with her Lord. When Jesus assures her that her brother will rise again, Hattie interrupts, assuring Jesus that she had learned that lesson in her Sunday School class at Calvary. "I know all about that Resurrection stuff," she would retort. But when Jesus offers a clarification, saying, "I am the Resurrection and the life, and he who believes in me, though he die, yet shall he live," Hattie has no farther rebuttal. So when Jesus asks her, "Do you believe this?" Hattie can say "Yes, Lord, I believe that you are the Christ, the Son of God."

It is altogether fitting and proper that this service of thanksgiving for Hattie's life should take place during the week of Easter. For it is in the "sure and certain hope" of that Resurrection, in which Hattie believed, that we commit her today. It is to the ever loving care and providence of that God who raised Jesus from the dead that we commend her soul. And it is our prayer that inspired by her long life and blessed example, we may be go from strength to strength in the service of Him who died for us and rose again, even Jesus Christ, our Lord. AMEN.

"Strength and dignity are her clothing."

MARGARET McCANN GARLAND (1926–2006)
Preached in Calvary Church, Pittsburgh
12 May 2006

Let not your hearts be troubled. (John 14:1)

THE PSALMIST TELLS US that a lifespan is reckoned as threescore years and ten, and, if we be especially fortunate, fourscore years (Ps 90:10). We gather here today, on the eve of what would have been the celebration of fourscore years for Margaret McCann Garland, to give thanks to Almighty God for her life, her witness, and her example. We come to this place where Peggy worshipped, this place where she dutifully served on the altar guild, this place where she brought beauty, excitement, and enthusiasm to her booths at the bazaar, to commend her to the never-failing care of the Bishop and Shepherd of our souls.

Peggy's life can be described in terms of relationships. I feel a certain kindred spirit with Peggy because we both grew up as only children at a time when that was considered a rare disease. Its cure was to seek surrogate siblings. Peggy did this with abandon, so much so that, this past week, several people told Peggy's family that they felt they had lost their best friend. Peggy believed, too, that it takes a village to raise a child. Family neighbors growing up were not Mrs. This or Mr. That to Peggy's children; they were Aunt Mary and Uncle Henry. Peggy must also have read the Epistle to the Hebrews, which encourages us to show hospitality to strangers because we may entertain angels unawares. As her daughters can attest, no one was an alien to Peggy's circle. Every friend or friend of a friend, every waif and stray was welcome in the Garland house, and an extra seat could always be found at Peggy's dining room table.

It is to Peggy's eternal credit that Gerry and Gayle did not grow up wracked with envy—because Peggy Garland's maternal love was not limited to her biological children. It was shared with the children she taught at St. Edmund's; it was dispensed on little ones at a pre-school she founded at Harvard; that love for children influenced all that she did as a board member at Winchester Thurston, her beloved alma mater, and it seems altogether fitting and proper that, just a few days before her death, a playground there was named in her honor.

Peggy was of the old school. She was resolute and strong-willed. She instilled cherished values in her grandchildren, William and Sarah, whom she adored, reminding them to give a strong handshake and always to look people in the eye. Never lacking courage, even when lying in great pain, she could muster the strength to say to those who inquired of her, "I'm doing so-so, but I'll be better tomorrow." We can well imagine that the writer of the Book of Proverbs might well have had Peggy in mind when he wrote:

> Strength and dignity are her clothing,
> And she laughs at the time to come.
> She opens her mouth with wisdom,
> And the teaching of kindness is on her tongue.
> (Prov 31:25–26)

That verse goes on to say, "Her children rise up and call her blessed, her husband, too, and he praises her" (Prov 31:28). Gray Garland has lost his companion, his soul-mate, his dearest friend, with whom he has spent the last fifty-eight years of his life. Ever solicitous, respectful, encouraging, and, yes, even at times obedient, he never forgot his wedding vows, even the phrase "in sickness and in health." In her final months, he never left her side, always offering comfort, affection, and compassion. When I came to anoint Peggy shortly before her death, I said to Gray, in a bungling effort to offer comfort, something like, "You have had a long and rich life together." But Gray's instinctive response was, "Yes, but I would still like to see Peggy recover." These were not the words of a man in denial, but the words of a loving husband, who never ceased being desirous of the very best for his wife.

In today's Gospel, Jesus says to his disciples, "Let not your hearts be troubled." He could have said, "Don't worry. Don't fret. Don't be preoccupied." He is telling the disciples, and us, that we can only find real hope and confidence by focusing on God rather than on ourselves. He is trying to convince us that only by being grounded in God can we be able to focus on God.

Sickness, disease, and pain can easily make us focus on ourselves. It is all too easy to rail at God and ask "Why me?" It is all too easy to feel sorry for ourselves and, in the process, make miserable the lives of those around us. But there is an alternative to this approach to suffering. It is summarized in a prayer that says, "Sanctify, O Lord, the sickness of your servant, that the sense of her weakness may add strength to her faith and seriousness to her repentance."

It is this latter path that Peggy took. Her suffering did not estrange her from God, but brought her closer to God. But she would be the first to admit that she was not able to do it alone. She was assisted by the faithful women who ministered faithfully to her in her final months, weeks, and days, who offered her spiritual solace as well as physical comfort. Her friends Anna, Terry, Connie, Linda, and Meg were no less than angels, for they were truly sent by God. It is they who enabled Peggy to experience what the church calls a holy death. And because she experienced a holy death, because she has learned to cast all her cares on Jesus, she is able to respond to her Lord's invitation. Peggy knows that one of those dwelling-places is for her. She knows that Jesus has prepared a place for her, and will take her to himself.

Towards the end of her earthly life, Peggy's body was frail, weak, and wracked with excruciating pain. But today, having shared in the resurrection of her Lord and Savior Jesus Christ, who has opened for her the gates of everlasting life, she has discarded that earthly shell and has exchanged it for a new and glorious body. Now Peggy can sing:

> O how glorious and resplendent,
> Fragile body shalt thou be,
> When endued with heav'nly beauty,
> Full of health, and strong, and free,
> Full of vigor, full of pleasure
> That shall last eternally. AMEN.

Grace, Gratitude, Generosity

ESTHER GRAFF CAMPBELL (1917–2006)
Preached in Calvary Church, Pittsburgh
3 June 2006

Do you believe this? (John 11:26)

TODAY, WE GATHER TO commit to the care of Almighty God our sister in Christ, Esther Graff Campbell. And as we do so, we would do well to reflect on those qualities of Esther's which made her not only special to us but also a holy presence in our lives.

Esther, first of all, exuded **Grace**. She was ever gracious, solicitous, and kind. In all her actions, her self-effacing humility shone through—so much so, that we felt we were in the presence of someone "just a little lower than the angels." Indeed, her actions often reminded us (although that would never have been Esther's intention) of just how much our own actions fail to measure up to that ideal. One of the last times I saw Esther was at Shadyside Hospital. The nurse was there, and she explained to me that she would have to subject Esther to a few tests to ascertain if her throat muscles enabled her to swallow properly. She gave Esther liquids and solids of various consistencies, and then would ask her to open her mouth, swallow hard, and even stick out her tongue. Then the nurse asked her if she knew her full name and if she knew what month and year it was. If she was perturbed that the nurse thought she was less than *compos mentis*, Esther didn't let on; she just answered each question accurately. Most of us, even if not old, frail, and in pain, would find these requests annoying and invasive of our "space." But Esther complied with each persistent request and even made a joke about how sticking out one's tongue is rude. When it was all over, Esther thanked the nurse profusely.

Esther also showed us what **Gratitude** is all about. It was my great privilege to take the Blessed Sacrament to Esther at Canterbury Place. Esther derived great comfort from receiving communion. It was, as the hymn reminds us, her "food and stay." But each time I visited her, she never failed to express her gratitude to me, for celebrating the eucharist for her, and to Calvary, from whose altar the sacrament came. Esther loved to worship the Lord in the beauty of holiness and few things gave her more pleasure than to be able to come to church and be part of the congregation. Only a week before her death, she actually apologized for not being able to make it to church and said that hopefully she would return soon.

Given these traits, it will come as no surprise that Esther also demonstrated great **Generosity**. She gave of her substance liberally and sacrificially to support her parish and to memorialize her beloved Everett.

And being gracious, grateful, and generous, she could say with the Blessed Apostle, "Who shall separate us from the love of Christ? Shall tribulation, or distress, or persecution, or famine, or nakedness or peril, or sword?" (Rom 8:35). And Esther, knowing how to take the bitter with the sweet, knowing, as Saint Paul says, how to be exalted and how to be abased, could resolutely answer with him, "For I am persuaded that neither death, nor life, nor angels, nor principalities, nor powers, nor things present, nor things to come . . . shall be able to separate us from the love of God, which is in Christ Jesus our Lord" (Rom 8:38–39).

In today's Gospel, we read the familiar story of Mary and Martha, those friends (or perhaps cousins) of Jesus whom he visited in Bethany whenever he wanted to chill out and just have a break from the arduous tasks of his ministry. On this occasion, he arrives shortly after the death of their brother, Lazarus. Martha, the busy, type-A sister, meets Jesus as he approaches the house, and said, "If you had been here, my brother would not have died."

This, by the way, according to many scholars, is not so much a rebuke as it is a lament. It is clear from what she says and does that she believes in Jesus as the agent of a gracious God. When told that her brother would rise again, Martha takes this to mean a future resurrection, but Jesus makes it clear that he himself is the resurrection and the life. When he asks Martha, "Do you believe this?" Martha responds that she does. Then she summons her sister, saying, "The Lord is calling you."

Mary and Martha are often presented as antithetical types— the hands-on, roll-up-her sleeves, whip-up-a-soufflé Martha versus the contemplative praying Mary. To the extent that that is accurate, Esther had a little of both sisters in her. Her theological acumen certainly would enable her, like Martha, to have a discussion about the Resurrection—or anything else—with her Lord, but her prayerful, reflective, and meditative character made it possible for her to sit at Jesus' feet as well.

Esther had said that she had hoped to return to church soon. And so she has. As sacramental people, people of signs and symbols, we will, at Esther's request, cense and sprinkle with holy water her earthly remains, in a kind of act of purification, of preparation. And as we receive Christ's Body and Blood, a "foretaste of glory divine," Esther has already been shown to her seat at that eternal banquet, experiencing that very glory to which we can only now aspire. She is in that "sweet and blessed country, the home of God's elect, that sweet and blessed country that eager hearts expect." She is, too, in that place where "sorrow and pain are no more, but life everlasting." And later today, she who was signed with the cross of Christ in her baptism, will be signed with the cross of Christ with a clump of dirt, in "sure and certain hope of the Resurrection."

Some years ago, in a Bible study class in my parish in Washington, someone asked the question, "Is it fair for a person who was never a practicing Christian, who never darkened a church door, to make a confession on his death bed and get into heaven just like the faithful Christian?" One parishioner, without batting an eyelash, said, "You have missed the point. Christianity is not a heavenly insurance policy, a vale of tears that you go through

before getting to heaven. The person who has been a lifelong practicing Christian *knew the joy of being a Christian.*" As this story
flashed in my mind, I thought of Esther Campbell, that perfect
amalgam of Mary and Martha, who, in her thoughts, words, and
deeds, showed that she enjoyed being a Christian, a child of God,
and an inheritor of the Kingdom of Heaven. May she rest in peace
and rise in glory. AMEN.

Happy Life, Happy Death

ELIZABETH FELIX PARRACK (1914–2006)
Preached in Calvary Church, Pittsurgh
8 June 2006

Let not your hearts be troubled. (John 14:1)

WE BEGAN THE SERVICE this afternoon with the hymn, "Joyful, joyful, we adore thee" for good reason. Mrs. Parrack often reminded me that her maiden name was Felix, and that "felix" means "happy." She believed she was aptly named because, she said, she had led a happy life. She felt blessed by her parents and by her beloved Edward, to whom she was married for fifty-seven blissful years. It might have been a longer marriage, by the way, except for what Elizabeth understood to be an unduly long courtship. In her inimitable fashion, she asked her suitor point blank when he would propose. Edward explained that he would do so as soon as his income reached the princely sum of two hundred dollars a month!

Elizabeth, too, was loved by her family. She felt cared for and doted on by her son, Ted, and grandsons, Taylor and Kevin, and there was a twinkle in her eye and a broad smile on her face when she talked about her great granddaughter, Aileene Elizabeth, and described the joy she experienced when she held her in her arms. So as we gather today to commit to God's eternal care our sister in Christ, Elizabeth Felix Parrack, it is not so much to mourn her loss as it is to celebrate her life. Elizabeth would want us, in the words of the hymn, to "melt the clouds of sin and sadness, drive the dark of doubt away."

Elizabeth's other source of strength was her faith. She was nurtured by the sacrament of Holy Communion, whether she came to church or the church came to her. That faith had seen her through much. She often related the story of how her parents were told that she would succumb to tuberculosis when she was a teenager. Later, her doctors feared she may not survive childbirth. More recently, she successfully battled against cancer—not once but twice. With each challenge, Elizabeth put herself in God's hands; she could, as the hymn reminds us, "take it to the Lord in prayer." It is no wonder, then, that her last request of me, scant hours before her death, was to pray for her. "Your prayers give me so much comfort," she said. I began to pray. But asking me to pray wasn't actually her last request. A few seconds into the prayer, Elizabeth asked if I wouldn't speak a little louder!

Today's Gospel contains these words: "Let not your hearts be troubled" (or, as another translation puts it, "Set your troubled hearts at rest. Trust in God always; trust also in me"). Elizabeth Parrack, throughout her life, has taken Jesus at his word. Not only was she comforted by Jesus' words of assurance, she believed, too, that Jesus had prepared a place for her. So now she can sing, "I know not, oh, I know not, what joys await me there; what radiancy of glory, that bliss beyond compare."

It is said that people often die in the same way that they lived. That was certainly true of Elizabeth Parrack. Even on her death bed, she exhibited those gracious, ladylike qualities which had long characterized her demeanor. Although weak and in pain, she received her callers with the same dignity and grace that she showed in her living room at Park Mansions, where so often she would insist that I have just a little sherry after our communion service. Even in the ICU, she could remark, "How nice of you to come to see me," then begin to recount how happy she was that so many new people had come to Calvary Church.

After this lively conversation, Elizabeth fell into a deep sleep. The monitor at her bedside indicated that her heart rate had plummeted. She was cold to the touch. Prayers were offered, psalms were recited, as we prepared for Elizabeth to breathe her last. But not yet, thank you very much. Elizabeth was not finished with her farewells. The party wasn't quite over. She awakened from her sleep, her heart rate was up, and she was noticeably warmer. There was more color in her cheeks. She apologized for having been asleep and launched into another round of conversations. And more to the point, she lived long enough to receive Taylor, Jennifer, and her great granddaughter and namesake. Then, Elizabeth could sing the *Nunc Dimittis* and enter into the nearer presence of Almighty God. These last hours of her life were like a coda at the end of a symphony. My dictionary defines "coda" as: "A few measures or a section added to the end of a piece of music to make a more effective ending."

And a more effective ending it was. In so doing, the aptly named Elizabeth Felix Parrack experienced a happy death at the end of a happy life. In dying, she taught us how to live. We can ask for no greater legacy than this. Well done, good and faithful servant!

"There must be something in the water"

SUSAN JOAN ALDER BOULDEN (1943–2007)
Preached in Calvary Church, Pittsburgh
31 March 2007

Blessed are the peacemakers, for they shall be called children of God. (Matt 5:9)

PITTSBURGH, IN THE SOUTHWEST corner of Pennsylvania, and Hull, in the northeast corner of England, have something in common. They are both cities found at the point where two rivers converge and flow into another. Here, as every schoolchild knows, the Allegheny and the Monongahela pour into the Ohio. Hull, the third largest port in England, is situated near that point where the Ouse and the Trent Rivers flow into the Humber. Judging from the people that that town has managed to produce over the centuries, I think we can safely say that there is indeed something in the water! In 1642, the townspeople of Hull, vehemently opposed to the notion of a Catholic king, were the first to shut their city gates, barring entry to the new monarch, Charles I. In the years following, in the midst of civil war, a royalist army occupied the rest of the north of England, but Hull remained a parliamentary outpost, defeating the king's forces not once but twice. About a century later, in Hull's High Street, was born her most famous son, William Wilberforce, who fought tirelessly to convince the English Parliament to abolish the slave trade, an event whose bicentenary we observe this year.

About a century after Wilberforce's death, Hull witnessed the birth of one of her most famous daughters, Susan Joan Alder. We who have come to this sacred place this morning knew her as Sue Boulden, and we gather to give thanks to Almighty God for that Yorkshire lass who must have drunk deeply from Hull's three rivers, for she, like her forebears, was feisty, energetic, and indefatigable. But she was also passionate about the causes she espoused, devout in the faith she professed, and loving to those of us privileged to be among her family and friends. Hours after her death last Tuesday night, someone wrote that she was not surprised that it was Sue's heart that gave out, because it was her heart that had for so many years worked overtime.

When we met with the family to discuss which lessons we would read today, someone suggested that the Beatitudes be the Gospel reading, and there was unanimous assent. It was as if we all sensed that Sue's life was a living out of the Beatitudes, which someone has called the Magna Carta of Christianity. The preacher could have picked any one of them and made a plausible argument for how Sue's life exemplified it—well, perhaps "blessed are the meek" would have been a bit of a stretch! So I ask that you meditate with me for a moment on the antepenultimate Beatitude, "Blessed are the peacemakers, for they shall be called children of God."

For us for whom the oft-repeated Beatitudes have run the risk of becoming platitudes, they perhaps have lost some of their significance. But that was certainly not the case with Jesus' original audience in first century Palestine. In stating that the peacemakers are blessed, Jesus was challenging conventional wisdom and turning it on its end. In those days, the warmongers were the blessed ones. Rome had conquered the known world; the corrupt Herod controlled Judea and was faring sumptuously every day, all the while ruling the Jewish peasants with an iron fist. Those who waged peace did not seem to receive any blessings at all.

Now first, what is this peace of which Jesus speaks? The Aramaic word that Jesus used was very close to the Hebrew "Shalom." Shalom—a theme that has, appropriately enough, figured prominently in the theology of our new Presiding Bishop—suggests far more than the absence of conflict but rather a peace that is found in wholeness, a wholeness of creation ordered by the Creator. This was the type of peace to which Sue was committed. Now someone has suggested that a better translation of the Greek would be "peace-doers" instead of "peacemakers." Somehow making peace might conjure up the idea of imposing it on other groups, whereas doing peace suggests that we start the process by having peace within ourselves, so that we can be in a better position to bring it to others. Sue, my brothers and sisters in Christ, was this kind of doer of peace.

Sue was a doer of peace between men and women. To describe Sue as a feminist would be to do her a disservice. She did not have to rely on using non-sexist language or cherishing a belief that men are domineering or insensitive. She depended on none of these things. Sue was just Sue. She didn't need an elaborate feminist theology to justify her confidence in the equality of women. Her actions spoke volumes, as anyone, male or female, who had a conversation with her, can attest. But just for fun, I wonder what it would have been like in Sue's EfM class when they studied First Corinthians. How I would have loved to hear her impassioned commentary on chapter 14, verse 35, "Women should be silent in the churches. For they are not permitted to speak, for they are subordinate." And I daresay Richard could attest that she seldom took Paul's advice in the next verse: "If there is anything they desire to know, let them ask their husbands at home."

Sue was a doer of peace between gay and straight. She could not comprehend the view, all too prevalent in some places, that gay people, by definition, suffer from some kind of pathology. She could not understand a theology that demanded that homosexual orientation was a cross to be borne valiantly by gays and lesbians. Mindful of a widespread attitude that homosexuality, to use Oscar Wilde's phrase, is "the love that dare not speak its name," she pushed for dialogue on the topic even when the powers-that-be were loath to allow it. In her last public utterance at a diocesan gathering, she criticized the church's endorsement of anti-gay legislation in the Province of Nigeria, and called the attention of the audience to the irreparable harm such laws cause for all people.

Sue was a doer of peace among racial groups. Growing up in Hull was her first exposure to what we now call multiculturalism, so when she arrived at Pitt many years later, it seemed very natural to Sue to join an overseas students' association. In moving about the church, she showed that she had no tolerance for racial bigotry in any form.

Sue was a doer of peace between progressive and conservative. Believing that all voices should be heard in this diocese, she was the driving force behind PEP. Her MO was never to lord it over others but rather to say, in the words of the prophet Isaiah, "Come let us reason together, though our sins be like scarlet" (Isa 1:18). Sue was often the one who extended the olive branch. When the "Hope and a Future" conference met in Pittsburgh, Sue purchased several copies of the newly published book called *Gays and the Future of Anglicanism* and had them delivered to all the primates in attendance. In carrying out her own brand of shuttle diplomacy between progressive and conservative, she was an original. A strong pro-life advocate, Sue was one of the few Episcopalians I know who was a card-carrying member of both Integrity and the National Organization of Episcopalians for Life, and, in the days when exhibits were allowed at diocesan convention, she would flit unabashedly between the two booths, handing out literature at each.

Sue was a doer of peace—period. We could spend the rest of the day recalling the random acts of kindness that sprang from her heart. It was she, after all, who organized the bus to Columbus for General Convention. And I shall ever be grateful to her for whipping up some proper English scones, complete with jam and clotted cream, for the anniversary of my ordination.

Last Sunday, as Sue, Richard, and I gathered in Sue's hospital room and offered up the holy eucharist, we thought we were giving her strength to get through the operation. And so we were. But, as it turned out, we were doing more; we were giving her the Viaticum, food for her journey to that place where sorrow and pain are no more, but life everlasting. One day short of sixty-four years is nowadays considered a short life, but before we start talking about "an untimely death," let us instead do two things. First, let us give thanks to God for what our sister Sue was able to do in the time allotted to her—which, by any reckoning, was far more than many people who outlive her by decades accomplish. Second, in this Great Relay Race which is the Christian life, let us vow to grab hold of the baton that Sue has passed on to us, so that we can carry on her valiant witness.

Everything that Sue did was grounded in a deep sense of justice. She envisioned a church where everybody—regardless of race, gender, sexual orientation, or any other distinction—would have a place at the table. Striving, especially in these fractious and troublous times, to help make that vision a reality is the very least we can do to honor Sue's blessed memory.

Rest eternal grant unto Sue, O Lord, and let light perpetual shine upon her. May her soul and the souls of all the faithful departed, through the mercy of God, rest in peace. AMEN.

"Aren't you going to give me a pledge card?"

ARDELLE DOUGLAS HOPSON (1927–2010)
Preached in Calvary Church, Pittsburgh
17 October 2010

Who are these clothed in white robes and where do they come from? (Rev 7:13)

ALMOST EXACTLY FOURTEEN YEARS ago, when I had been at Calvary for only a few weeks, I received a message that a Mrs. Ardelle Hopson had made an appointment to see me. The purpose of her visit was to discuss transferring into Calvary from the parish to which she then belonged. This, of course, is music to a rector's ears, especially those of a new rector, and I eagerly looked forward to our meeting.

At the agreed upon time, the said Mrs. Hopson arrived (punctually, of course) and, in the course of our conversation, shared with me something of her spiritual journey. She took pride in being a cradle Episcopalian and spoke fondly of having been nurtured in the faith at the old Holy Cross in the Hill District. She mentioned her current parish and indicated that, for some time, she and Al had become increasingly unhappy there, pointing out that the last straw was when the rector did away with the choir! (A choir-less church, as far as Mrs. Hopson was concerned, gave new definition to oxymoron!) It was then that the Hopsons set out on a quest for a new spiritual home, and Calvary Church has been richly blessed by the fact that they chose to come here. The Hopsons loved Calvary, and threw themselves into the work of the parish. They joined the choir and Ardelle was soon a member of the Vestry. They took delight in attending as many services and events as they could—be it Shrove Tuesday pancakes, a Mozart Requiem, or the visit of the Archbishop of Canterbury—and, yes, were often the first to arrive. Their faithful attendance inflicted undue wear and tear on them when they had to commute from Plum, so I insisted that they move closer—which they did.

During our first meeting, Mrs. Hopson made it very clear that, although they might begin attending Calvary right away, their membership should not become effective until January first. The reason was simple. She had made a pledge to her old parish for the current year, which she had every intention of honoring. I thanked Mrs. Hopson profusely, and expressed how happy I was that she and her husband were joining Calvary—and Calvary's choir. The session having come to an end—or so I thought—I rose, but Mrs. Hopson did not budge. She looked up at me and asked, "Aren't you going to give me a pledge card?"

Well, Ardelle got a pledge card that day and, needless to say, has filled one out every year since. She will always be remembered at Calvary as Miss Stewardship, on account of her impassioned testimonials (delivered every year, during the Annual Appeal), which inspired many of her fellow parishioners to dig a little deeper in their pockets than they might otherwise have. Ardelle believed in putting your money where your mouth is.

As we come together in the church Ardelle loved so much to commit her soul to a loving Creator, we listen to words from the Revelation of Saint John the Divine. It is a question asked of John by one of the elders: "Who are these clothed in white robes and where do they come from?" But the elder answers his own question: "These are they who have come out of the great tribulation; they have washed their robes and made them white in the blood of the Lamb" (Rev 7:14). This is one of the many Biblical descriptions of what heaven will be like. They are comfortable and reassuring words, depicting the heavenly realms as a place where we needn't worry about the vicissitudes of life with which we must contend on earth.

A few weeks ago, I was on the 7:30 p.m. flight from LaGuardia to Pittsburgh. It left the gate at 9:30, after which the pilot announced that we were Number 53 in the departure queue, which translated into a wheels-up of about 11 o'clock. My seatmate prophesied that we would be best friends by the time we arrived in Pittsburgh. Well, not exactly. Once he found out what I did for a living, he changed the topic from the weather to religion. (Yes, this is an occupational hazard of the reverend clergy.) Specifically, he was concerned about his father, a lapsed Christian, who was terminally ill, having just been told he had less than a year to live. My seatmate said that his father was concerned about what heaven would be like. He was probably not pleased with my answer. I told him that his father should better be concerned with making peace with his loved ones, mending fences, and putting the last months of his life to the best possible use. It was an exercise in futility, I suggested, to worry about what heaven was like; that should be left to God. His father, I think, was concerned that his deeds may have disqualified him from entrance into the Pearly Gates, and therefore consignment to the "other place."

My seatmate's father, like so many of us, saw Christianity as a celestial insurance policy, whose premiums are doing good works, being kind to your neighbor, and the like. Too many people fail to grasp that the Christian faith is its own reward. We do good works not to appease a Santa-Claus God who rewards us according to whether we're naughty or nice. We do such things because they are our bounden duty and service, because we are members of Christ's church militant here in earth.

I think Ardelle got it. She understood what the Christian life was all about. She told me that she didn't know exactly what awaited her, but that that was all right. She could live with that uncertainty because she took comfort in knowing that she had done all in her power to touch the lives of those around her. Like the Blessed Apostle, she could say "I have fought the good fight, I have finished the course, I have kept the faith" (2 Tim 4:7).

Ardelle Hopson was a type-A personality, always busy, always task-oriented. She was thorough and meticulous. Many may be unaware of the fact that she kept a detailed file on the trials and tribulations of our Diocese, which we euphemistically dubbed "the recent unpleasantness." Ardelle assembled two large volumes containing clippings, sermons, press releases, *Agape* articles, and court decisions. These proved to be of invaluable assistance to Walter DeForest in the preparation of our legal case. Ardelle, to say the least, was straightforward and unambiguous. She spoke her mind to all who would listen and to a few who wouldn't. Needless to say, she could speak truth to power, especially if that power had a mitre on his head. She seemed to take her marching orders from the prophet Ezekiel, who said, "Whether they hear or refuse to hear, they will know that a prophet has been among them" (Ezek 2:5).

In the early stages of her final illness, Ardelle constantly expressed a desire to get back to her routine. She wanted to return to her duties on the counting team, on the stewardship committee, and on Diocesan Council, with her social club and her sorority. But when it finally became clear that such re-entry would be unlikely, she sat down at her computer and dutifully and resolutely wrote letters to all of the organizations with which she was affiliated, informing them that she would no longer be able to serve.

And near the end, as we prayed together, we agreed that her prayer would be to let go and let God. Two days before her death, having made the decision not to employ extraordinary means to prolong her life, she could tell me and Claudette that she was at peace, content to put herself in the Lord's hands. Perhaps, in so doing, she reflected on the words of John Mason Neale's great hymn:

> There is the throne of David, and there, from care released,
> The shout of them that triumph, the song of them that feast;
> And they, who with their Leader, have conquered in the fight,
> Forever and forever are clad in robes of white.[6]

6. Neale, "Jerusalem the Golden."

"This is the best party in town!"

AUDREY HILLMAN HILLIARD (1925–2015)
Preached in Calvary Church, Pittsburgh
14 October 2011

See what great love the Father has lavished on us, that we should be called children of God! (1 John 3:1)

THREE YEARS AGO, AUDREY and Tommy Hilliard celebrated their sixtieth wedding anniversary—and of course, there was a grand party! Children, grandchildren, relatives, and friends descended on Pittsburgh to join in the festivities. Sister Sally even sported the bonnet and sash that were part of her bridesmaid's ensemble in 1948. I composed a prayer for the occasion, and Audrey and Tommy liked it so much, I asked Ken Smith, our director of communications, to make it into a card, which was duly framed and festively wrapped. I called at the Hilliards' home on Inverness one afternoon to deliver it. Tommy wasn't there, but Audrey warmly received me and thanked me for the gift, which she unwrapped with the enthusiasm of a toddler opening a Christmas present. But when all the tissue paper was removed, Audrey looked up at me, all smiles, and simply asked "What is it?" She then gently reminded me that her eyesight had been failing for some time.

I had forgotten. And the reason I had forgotten is that throughout her illness, Audrey did not exhibit one shred of self-pity; she did not for one minute rail against God asking him "Why me?"—and, thankfully, she showed neither indignation nor exasperation toward her obtuse rector. Like the Apostle Paul, she knew how to be exalted and how to be abased. The radiant smile for which she was famous lit up a room and brought unbridled joy to all in her orbit. Nearly every Sunday, at coffee hour, she could be depended upon to say one of two things—either, "Isn't Calvary a wonderful place?" or, "This is the best party in town!" And she knew whereof she spoke. Marguerite and James Hillman brought her to Calvary's font to be baptized; the third bishop of Pittsburgh laid hands on her in this place in the sacrament of Confirmation, and it was in front of this rood screen that she promised to love, honor, and cherish—but I think not obey—Thomas Jones Hilliard Jr. as long as they both shall live. So today, we have come full circle, as we return to this hallowed place, to commend the soul of Audrey Hilliard to a loving and compassionate God, who gave her life and who has preserved her in the faith for more than fourscore years.

Audrey began her Christian life in the family pew, where Mrs. Hillman kept a stern eye on her four daughters. It was there that manners and decorum, as well as piety, were instilled. I remember Audrey telling me that, after arriving home one Sunday, her mother made her write one hundred times, "I will not remove my gloves with my teeth." Audrey, in her Christian nurture, would have learned the Catechism, with the question: "What is your bounden duty and service as a Christian?" to which the answer is: "My bounden duty and service is to worship God every Sunday in his church, and to work, pray, and give for the spread of Christ's Kingdom." But to this list, Audrey would probably add "give back." Audrey took seriously our Lord's command "From those to whom much is given, much will be required." Audrey's family had instilled in her what the world calls *noblesse oblige*. She did not subscribe to the idea that outreach means "keeping others out of our reach." Rather, she believed that it means hands-on involvement with those to whom she sought to minister. For this reason, helping to found the Calvary Lincoln After School Program and supporting it financially were not enough. Audrey was intimately involved, making snacks, helping with arts and crafts, and escorting the children to the Carnegie.

Three days ago, a committee made up of Tommy, the Hilliard children, and the reverend clergy of Calvary Church sat around a table and tried to put together a service which would be reflective of Audrey and speak to her spirit. When we considered Scripture readings, there was immediate agreement on the epistle from 1 John. Listen to it in modern translation:

> Little does the world know of the happiness of the real followers of Christ. Little does the world think that these poor, humble, despised ones are favorites of God, and will dwell in heaven. The children of God must walk by faith, and live by hope. The children of God will be known, and be made manifest by likeness to their Head. They shall be transformed into the same image, by their view of him. (1 John 3:1)

I believe there was consensus around this passage because those at that table believed that, although the world may not know of the happiness of the real followers of Christ, although the world does not recognize the least, the lost, and the last as his favorites, Audrey certainly did. Audrey was a people person. Her family says that she inherited from her mother a brand of Southern hospitality that always ensured that everybody has a place at the table. And by virtue of being around that table, we become like the Christ whom we imitate. Our little committee saw this passage as Audrey's spiritual resume. They saw in Audrey one who took seriously the words of the Baptismal Covenant, to "seek and serve Christ in all persons, loving your neighbor as yourself," and to "strive for justice and peace among all people, and respect the dignity of every human being."

Now, I have an announcement to make this morning to Tim, Connie, Elsie, Peggy, and Jamie. You have another brother. Audrey adopted me fifteen years ago when she chaired the search committee that called me to be rector. Like a good mother, she has consistently demonstrated her love, her affection, and her appreciation, all the while encouraging me in my work and lavishing me with unmerited praise. I will leave it to history to assess the ministry of Calvary's fifteenth rector, but I will say to you this morning something which I have said to Audrey more than once. Even if I had not been called, I would sing the praises of Audrey's search committee for its flawless process. While many of my colleagues going through the process have been treated in ways that vary from cavalier to flippant to indifferent, Mrs. Hilliard ran a tight ship. Her committee laid out the process, adhered to the schedule it had put forward, apologized for any changes to it, and respected the integrity of each candidate. If she was as assiduous in her other endeavors as she was in this project, it is no wonder that she has made such a lasting impact on this community.

Today we gather to give thanks for the life of a woman whom the author of Proverbs had in mind when he wrote: "Who can find a virtuous woman? Her price is far above rubies" (Prov 31:10). To what can we attribute her great qualities? First, her marriage for more than six decades to Tommy Hilliard. If you watched the slide show yesterday and saw that couple playing Mary and Joseph in the pageant, riding a camel in Egypt, or enjoying a kiss at Tommy's birthday party, it was clear that they are and always have been very much in love. Second, Audrey was supported by the love of her family. She took easily to the role of matriarch, nurturing and caring for each generation, who, again in the words of Proverbs, will "rise up and call her blessed" (Prov 31:28). Finally, her church. She found strength both in the community of the faithful of this parish and in the nourishment of the sacraments. Four days before her death, I had the privilege of administering Holy Communion to Audrey for the last time. When she thanked me, I simply said that as she had faithfully come to church for so long, now that she was not able to do so, the church would come to her. "Is that a deal?" I asked. "That's a deal!" she replied. And now, an even greater deal awaits Audrey. One of the many mansions in her Father's house has her name on it.

Rest eternal grant unto Audrey, O Lord, and may light perpetual shine upon her. May her soul and the souls of all the faithful departed through the mercy of God rest in peace and rise in glory. AMEN.

"I am not devastated!"

JOANNE ROSS WILDER (1942–2011)
Preached in Calvary Church, Pittsburgh
29 November 2011

Let not your hearts be troubled. (John 14:1)

I HAVE COME TO the conclusion—admittedly not a remarkable one—that we go through life not really knowing our neighbors and those with whom we come into regular contact. We get to know various facets of their lives, perhaps only those facets necessary to enable us to interact with them in those capacities that bear direct relevance to our relationship. And so it is that obituaries serve to shine a light on those aspects of people's lives of which we had been blissfully ignorant. Shortly after I came to Calvary, I officiated at the funeral of a founder of a prestigious, carriage-trade law firm in this city. Upon reading his obituary, I learned that he had taken a leave of absence from that firm to volunteer his time in Mississippi, conducting voter registration drives for disenfranchised African Americans. Who knew? Likewise, Joanne Wilder's obituary, reporting as it did her national renown as an attorney, educator, and author may well have come as a surprise to her fellow parishioners here, who saw her across the aisle at the eight o'clock mass or who bought a book from her when she volunteered in the Calvary Bookstore.

There was one thing in Joanne's obituary that did not come as a surprise—that she worked as a fashion model while she was an undergraduate. Joanne never lost her sense of style, her flair. While she could never be called flashy, she was distinctive, a class act. A sense of class characterized every aspect of her life, a life which many would say ended far too soon.

I almost used the word "untimely" to describe Joanne's death, but I don't use that word anymore. I believe that, instead of zeroing in on the quantity of life, giving people credit, as a friend of mine put it, for drawing breath and a paycheck, we should learn to concentrate on the quality of life, and give people credit for what they have been able to accomplish in the time allotted to them. At life's end, each of us should be able to say, in the words of an old hymn, "If I can help somebody along the way, then my living shall not be in vain." Whose lives have we touched? What difference have we made? Is the planet a better place because we have trod on its surface? By these criteria, the life of Joanne Ross Wilder was long and rich indeed, and we can only give thanks that God saw fit to share her with us for a period just shy of the biblical lifespan of threescore years and ten.

Joanne did indeed leave the world a better place than she found it. She was one of a rare breed who were able not only to ply their trade, but to impart to others the skills they had learned. More importantly, Joanne found time to give back, to be an advocate for the voiceless and powerless, be they rape victims or women caught in the vortex of especially acrimonious divorce proceedings. She gave back in simple ways, too, such as serving on the parish council of this congregation. It was there that she had the rare experience of losing a case—she tried to convince her colleagues that they should recommend placing Bibles in the pews—a hard-sell for Episcopalians!

Today's Gospel lesson contains these words: "Let not your hearts be troubled" (or, as another translation puts it, "Set your troubled hearts at rest"). Jesus uses these words as he speaks to his disciples in a moment of crisis. Gathered together in the Upper Room, he tells them that he will be departing from them, but he admonishes them, "Let not your hearts be troubled." The disciples didn't know or understand where he would be going, and it was not at all certain if they could go with him. But Jesus tells them nevertheless, "Let not your hearts be troubled." Jesus himself had cause for concern; he knew that one of his disciples would be a traitor, and that even Peter, his chief lieutenant, would deny he even knew his Lord. Yet he insists on encouraging them with the words, "Let not your hearts be troubled."

Everything seemed to be on the verge of collapse, but Jesus told them not to worry, not to fear, not to fret. Jesus was warning them of the type of fear that leads to paralysis, when we worry so much (often in the time of crisis), we become so depressed, that we are unable to function. Worry, as someone once said, is like rocking in a rocking chair; it gives you something to do, but it doesn't get you anyplace.

I think this verse is especially appropriate this morning because we can hear Joanne saying these words. Joanne did not let her heart be troubled. Joanne didn't fret. She didn't worry. She took things in his stride. She was virtually unflappable. It was Joanne whom Rudyard Kipling had in mind when he wrote:

> You can keep your head when all about you
>
> Are losing theirs and blaming it on you.[7]

How do I know this? Because three weeks ago, Joanne called me to say that she was dying and she wanted me to come over to plan her funeral. The statement was neither frantic nor alarmist; it was just matter-of-fact, as if she had just read the words from the burial office: "In the midst of life we are in death." The next morning, as I sat at her side, taking notes, she very clearly gave me instructions as to what would be done today—the speakers, the music, the rite. Then, she said, "I have done everything in life that I wanted to do." Would she, could she have done more? Of course. But she expressed gratitude that she had been given the grace—and the time—to accomplish what she had. She was at peace.

Now I often comment that the disciples are frequently obtuse; they sometimes just don't get it. Even in today's Gospel, Thomas doesn't understand Jesus' metaphorical language, and asks, "How

7. Kipling, "If," 170.

63

can we know the way?" (John 14:5). Well, the reverend clergy, lamentably, are prone to inherit this unfortunate trait. When Joanne had finished her soliloquy, I searched my mind for a word of comfort I could offer her; I wanted to assure her that she would be missed by her church family. So what did I say? I said, "Joanne, we are all as devastated as you are." As soon as the words fell from my lips, I realized they constituted probably the dumbest thing I had said in forty years of priestly life. Clearly, Joanne had come to the same conclusion, but she was characteristically gracious. She mustered all the strength she could command and announced, "I am *not* devastated." She was right, of course. She was not devastated. Her heart was not troubled. She had fought the good fight and finished the course. She was ready. She had put her house in order. She could now sing in the words of the great hymn:

> I fear no foe, with thee at hand to bless;
> Ills have no weight, and tears no bitterness.
> Where is death's sting? Where, grave, thy victory?
> I triumph still, if thou abide with me.

So today, we gather in this hallowed place, a place where Joanne had found spiritual solace, and we commend her to the never-failing care of a merciful Savior. We know that Joanne, far from being devastated, has triumphed, and would wish that we share in her triumph. The suddenness of her departure will make this a difficult task, indeed, for Bruce and Charlie, and for Cynthia, Diane, and David. It will be hard for her friends and colleagues, but it is our prayer that they will accept the invitation contained in that great hymn:

> Come ye disconsolate, where'er ye languish,
> Come to the mercy seat, fervently kneel,
> Here bring your wounded hearts, here tell your anguish,
> Earth has no sorrow that heav'n cannot heal.

May she rest in peace and rise in glory. AMEN.

"The good among the great."

PAULA WELLES ORR (1927–2012)
Preached in Calvary Church, Pittsburgh
8 May 2012

Let not your hearts be troubled. (John 14:1)

FORTY YEARS AGO, WHEN I was a student at Cambridge University, Claudette and I were invited—make that "summoned"—to a reception at the Master's Lodge of St. John's College. At the appointed hour, we entered the vast baronial hall which had stood on that spot for more than five hundred years. The Master's butler, in full livery (holding, in one hand, the Master's mace—on top of which was a great silver eagle), bowed to us as he accepted our invitation card. He then knocked his mace on the oaken floor and, with a voice that can only be described as stentorian, announced our names. Another knock ensued, and we were ushered in to be received by the Master of the College and his good wife. Each time I have related that story over the past four decades, I have added that, in the category of grand entrances—and I have made a few—nothing could ever top that!

I was mistaken. Last Friday, I called at the Orr residence on Aylesboro. Welles preceded me into his mother's bedroom. He leaned over her frail form, which had already assumed a fetal position, and whispered, "Mother, Harold Lewis is here to see you." The immediate response from the bed was "Oh, good!" With those two barely audible syllables, I was ushered into Poosie's presence, and I don't remember ever being more warmly welcomed anyplace. Being ushered into the presence of the Master of St. John's, amidst all the trappings of the Empire, could not hold a candle to the sense of privilege I felt being ushered into the presence of Paula Welles Orr on the last full day of her earthly life, which just happened to be her eighty-fifth birthday.

Poosie's obituary described her as "a lifelong student." True to form, she wanted to continue her learning experience unto the very end. A book of daily meditations by the Presbyterian theologian Frederick Buechner lay on her nightstand, and she asked me to open it to the entry for May 4th and to read it to her, which I did. There followed some prayers, an anointing, and a brief conversation on random topics. These included birthday wishes, a word or two about St. Monica—whose feast day it happened to be—and crossword puzzles. I was always insanely jealous of Poosie, who had managed to complete the Sunday Times puzzle before the 11 o'clock service while I was still slaving over a hot altar! Poosie even made a joke about the bird singing outside her window, suggesting that the little creature had followed her home from the hospital.

One of the last things she said to me, smiling as she said so, was "I am on my way." It was clear that she was ready, had made her peace with God, and that she would experience a holy death. It just doesn't get any better than this!

Today's Gospel lesson contains these words: "Let not your hearts be troubled" (or as another translation puts it, "Set your troubled hearts at rest"). Jesus uses these words as he speaks to his disciples in a moment of crisis. Gathered together in the Upper Room, he tells them that he will be departing from them, but he admonishes them, "Let not your hearts be troubled." The disciples didn't know or understand where he would be going, and it was not at all certain if they could go with him. But Jesus tells them nevertheless, "Let not your hearts be troubled." Jesus himself had cause for concern; he knew that one of his disciples would be a traitor, and that even Peter, his chief lieutenant, would deny he even knew his Lord. Yet he insists on encouraging them with the words, "Let not your hearts be troubled."

Everything seemed to be on the verge of collapse, but Jesus told them not to worry, not to fear, not to fret. Jesus was warning them of the type of fear that leads to paralysis, when we worry so much (often in the time of crisis), we become so depressed, that we are unable to function. Worry, as someone once said, is like rocking in a rocking chair; it gives you something to do, but it doesn't get you anyplace.

I think this verse is especially appropriate this morning because we can hear Poosie saying these words. Poosie did not let her heart be troubled. Poosie didn't fret. She didn't worry. She took things in his stride. She was virtually unflappable. It was Poosie whom Rudyard Kipling had in mind when he wrote:

> You can keep your head when all about you
>
> Are losing theirs and blaming it on you.[8]

I think Poosie did not worry because she didn't have time to worry. Poosie Orr is one of the people described in a book called *Good Among the Great: 19 Traits of the Most Admirable, Creative, and Joyous People*. In it, the author, Donald Van de Mark, cites several characteristics of Poosie's personhood which effectively precluded the possibility of fretting.[9]

First, Poosie knew how to be creative, and she shared this gift with her children and those around her. Creativity, to Poosie, was the fundamental way that human beings respond to God, their Creator. "It's very important that people use their hands somehow," she said. "I think we're meant to. Whether we're painting, or cooking, or sewing, or digging, I just think there's something very vital about using your hands." Next, Poosie knew how to laugh. Humor was a trait she deemed indispensable to the human psyche. She believed that good, healthy folk who don't take themselves too seriously laugh *at* themselves and *with* others. Moreover, Poosie knew how to love. Love, to Poosie, isn't dependent or mired in need or compulsion. Real love is interdependent, allowing each person the fullest expression of themselves, free of need or demand.

8. Kipling, "If," 170.

9. See Van de Mark, *Good Among the Great.*

But I would like to add one trait not specifically mentioned by Mr. Van de Mark. Poosie knew how to pray. When her children came by yesterday to plan this service, they brought Poosie's Bible. Its pages were dog-eared, discolored, and smudged. It obviously had been read, re-read, studied, and prayed over for decades. Comments and notes filled virtually ever margin—maybe they were insights gleaned in an EfM class or from a book of devotional readings. She exercised great care, as well, in choosing the lessons to be read today, and we know that she was greatly comforted by this morning's Psalm, which speaks of the omnipresence of the Almighty:

> Whither shall I go from thy spirit, or whither shall I flee from thy presence? If I climb up to heaven, thou art there; if I make my bed in hell, thou art there also. (Psalm 139:7–8)

Today, we give thanks for a woman whom her children will rise up and call blessed, for a woman whose life has been an inspiration to others—her children and grandchildren, generations of her students, and her fellow pilgrims at Calvary Church. I was not surprised when I read in Poosie's obituary that she had been an ice-skating instructor. The skills needed—artistry, grace, and creativity, coupled with precision and timing, all undergirded by faith, very much sum up the gifts of this faithful servant of God whom we now commend to God's care. Poosie has indeed climbed up to heaven, where, as our Lord reminds us, he has prepared a special place for her. AMEN.

"Tent or no tent?"

ELSIE HILLIARD HILLMAN (1925–2015)
Preached in Calvary Church, Pittsburgh
19 September 2015

Behold, I make all things new. (Rev 21:5)

As I was completing my seminary training, the final examination in Holy Scripture was an oral one, and there was only one question: "Mr Lewis," announced the examining chaplain, "It is said that the Bible begins in a garden and ends in a city. Comment on the role of the city in Holy Scripture." It was, at one level, a trick question. For the holy city seen by John in the book of Revelation was, in the mind of its author, a replica of the Garden of Eden before the Fall. And nor was that holy city merely a vision of heaven but rather a vision of heaven here on earth, for we read: "I saw the Holy City, the new Jerusalem, *coming down out of heaven from God*" (Rev 21:2). It is in this context that Jesus pronounces, "Behold, I am making all things new."

My friends, as we gather this morning to give thanks for the life and witness of Elsie Hilliard Hillman and to commit her to the never-failing care of her Creator and Redeemer, I put to you that Elsie was committed throughout her life to assisting her Lord in making all things new, by making it possible for all of God's people on "this fragile earth, our island home" to catch a glimpse of that holy city Jerusalem. (And I needn't remind you that the New Testament word translated as "city" is *polis*, which, as my Greek

69

professor would say, comes from our word "politics.") It is in this sense, therefore, that Elsie was an exemplary political organizer, a consummate political activist, indeed, the quintessential political animal. It was her passion, her ministry, her life's work.

Elsie took Jesus at his word when he said, "If you have done it unto the least of these my brothers and sisters, you have done it unto me" (Matt 25:40). This is why, when AIDS was considered a scourge and a punishment against the gay community, Elsie not only delivered baskets of food to people dying from the disease but remained to eat with them.

Elsie believed Jesus when he promised that everyone's birthright was "to have life and to have it abundantly" (John 10:10). This is why she was unstinting in her labors to empower those too often at the margins of our society, notably women and African Americans—not with handouts but with introductions and endorsements to those in positions of power.

Elsie trusted Jesus when he said, "To those to whom much is given, much will be required" (Luke 12:48). This is why she and Henry have been paragons of philanthropy in this community and have set an example to follow for three more generations in their family.

Elsie learned these lessons in this very church, where she was baptized nearly nine decades ago and where she continued to be nurtured in the faith—driving herself to the 8 o'clock Eucharist Sunday by Sunday in a little car with an elephant on the hood—although some people insist that it was a donkey!

One particular story comes to mind as a parable of Elsie's life of selfless service and generosity of spirit. Several years ago, we learned that the Archbishop of Canterbury would be visiting Calvary Church, and we began to organize a series of events for him and Lady Carey. My first official act was to phone Elsie. I asked her if she and Henry could possibly host a dinner at their home to welcome our special visitors to Pittsburgh, even though, since that visit was to occur in August, it would necessitate their flying home from Canada, where the Hillmans spent the summer. Without a moment's hesitation, Elsie said, "Of course!" and, in the same breath, asked, "Tent or no tent?" She answered her own question and decided on a tent, and, when the gala evening arrived, one hundred and fifty guests partook of a sumptuous supper under an *air-conditioned* tent on the Hillmans' expansive lawn, the guests at each table having been chosen and seated by Mrs. Hillman herself to ensure maximum harmony and complementarity.

This was a microcosm of Elsie's *polis*, a tent under which "all sorts and conditions" of people can find a comfortable place of welcome, dignity, and recognition. I believe that Elsie Hilliard Hillman, in her ardent hope to fashion anew the holy city—God's *polis*—here on earth, might well have been inspired by the words of the great hymnwriter James Russell Bowie:

> Give us, O God, the strength to build
> The city that hath stood
> Too long a dream, whose laws are love,
> Whose ways are brotherhood,
> And where the sun that shineth is
> God's grace for human good.
>
> Already in the mind of God
> That city riseth fair:
> Lo, now its splendor challenges
> The souls that greatly dare—
> Yes, bids us seize the whole of life
> And build its glory there.[10]

10. Bowie, "O Holy City," 494.

III: ALL SORTS AND CONDITIONS OF MEN

"It is well with my soul."

CURTIS WINFIELD SISCO Jr., Priest (1958–1992)
Preached in the Church of St. Andrew & St. Monica,
Philadelphia
28 November 1992

> In the sight of the unwise they seemed to die ... and their
> going from us is utter destruction, but they are at peace.
> (Wis 3:2–3)

FIVE AND A HALF years—a mere sixty-six months ago, when I first
had the privilege of mounting this pulpit, it was on the joyous occasion when we gathered to set apart and ordain our well-beloved
brother in Christ, Curtis Winfield Sisco Jr., as a priest in Christ's
holy catholic church. Today, an even greater privilege has been ac-
corded me—as I preach at this solemn mass of requiem at which
we commend Curtis to the provident and never-failing care of
Jesus Christ, the Bishop and Shepherd of our souls, in whose eternal high priesthood it was Curtis's joy to share.

Although I have known for several months, since the day that
Curtis humbled me by requesting that I function in this capacity, that this honor would befall me, I gave no thought whatsoever
to what I would say until Monday, when Cutis breathed his last.
There are probably two reasons for this. One is the same reason
that people have for not making wills: I was in denial. The second
is that I simply did not know what I would say. Instead, I took Jesus
at his word when he assured us that, when it came time to speak,

75

he would give us the power of utterance. I prayed that God would be merciful to me as he had been with the prophet Jeremiah and would put the words into my mouth.

For in times like these, words are all that we have. Inadequate though words may be, in and of themselves, they are expected to soothe our pain, lessen our sorrow, assuage our guilt, and make sense out of senselessness. Curtis's father, who gave his son life and his name thirty-four years ago, hopes that the words of a prayer will give him some confidence. Bernie, who herself has been immeasurably touched by her brother's ministry, prays that a friend's expression of sympathy will comfort her; Cecil, who, like Solomon, can say that his brother's going from him is "utter destruction" hopes that a homiletic offering, perhaps, can provide some explanation for his great loss; Curtis's beloved nana, to whom he presented a rose in this church on the day of his ordination, is hopeful that the words of a hymn might lift her from her devastation.

And all of us, friends and colleagues, expect words to work miracles today. Because when a man dies young, as Curtis has, our pain, our guilt, our disbelief, and, yes, our anger are greater than usual. For although we mouth the majestic words of the burial office, "In the midst of life we are in death"; although we listen to that beautifully cadenced prayer that reads, "Make us, we beseech thee, deeply sensible of the shortness and uncertainty of life"; yet in our heart of hearts we believe that our timetable is the one to which we should adhere, not God's; and when a person's life falls too sort of the Psalmist's threescore years and ten, we fly in God's face. You see, events like Curtis's death remind us that, while we may have our respective master plans, they do not always jibe with the Master's Plan. And it is for this very reason that we, who in our arrogance decide which deaths are "timely" and which are "untimely," are instructed by the church with these words from the book of The Wisdom of Solomon:

> For though they be punished in the sight of men, yet is their hope full of immortality. And having been chastised, they shall be greatly rewarded: for God proved them, and found them worthy for himself. (Wis 3:4–5)

What is Curtis's legacy to our church? First of all, Curtis leaves us a deep and abiding understanding of the nature and dignity of the priesthood. Curtis was a priest's priest. Nobody can remember when Curtis was not a priest. That is because what Bishop Bartlett and the rest of us did in this church five years ago was merely to recognize officially that which had been his identity from the start. "Before I formed you in the womb," said God to Curtis, "I knew you for my own; before you were born I consecrated you." There are many clergy for whom the priesthood is something that they do; for our departed brother Curtis it was something that he was. He was priest in every bone, in every sinew. When Curtis said he would keep you in his prayers, we knew that was not some mere cliché. When Curtis celebrated mass, it was as natural to him as breathing. When he preached, his listeners knew at once that Jesus was no stranger to him.

Secondly, Curtis bequeaths to us a love of the liturgy. And let the record show that he was no garden-variety "spike"—one who grooves on bells and smells for their own sake. He understood the deeper significance of every gesture, every vestment, every rubric, and saw each as it was originally intended, a vessel of God's grace. For this reason, Curtis was truly in his element when he was or-chestrating worship, for he never lost sight of the larger picture, the ultimate purpose of worship—to bring heaven down to earth—to grant us in our earthly pilgrimage a vision of the heavenly Jerusa-lem. He was the quintessential master of ceremonies. His impos-ing presence notwithstanding, he could move about a sanctuary with dignity and grace. A nod of the head, a glance, a gentle prod-ding at the elbow, all of which was imperceptible to the faithful in the pews, would instill obedience, reverence, and holy fear in the hearts of acolytes, priests, and even greater prelates—and would invariably achieve the desired result. No one can forget the wor-ship services at the UBE conference last year; people thronged the church each evening to see if Curtis could outdo what had trans-pired the night before, and they were not disappointed. When I visited him in New Orleans on the night before he returned to Philadelphia, he said to me that God had had a sense of humor for having spared him for the deanship of the UBE conference, which Curtis described as his "swan song." But that was not to be; God spared him to coordinate the music and worship for the glorious mass less than three weeks ago, which was the culmination of the celebration of the two-hundred-year anniversary of the black presence in the Episcopal Church

Thirdly, Curtis Winfeld Sisco Jr. was a teacher. His brother and sister clergy called, wrote, and faxed him regularly when they wanted to do an evensong or a Corpus Christi procession; they called him when they wanted to know if they were entitled to wear piping on their cassock or biretta and, if so, which color. The answer was always on the tip of tongue; and, if not, it was at his fingertips, for he know exactly what missal, sacramentary, or manual to consult. Being an accomplished musician as well, he could do workshops on worship which left the faithful not only enlightened but inspired. He taught all of us, too, on the editorial committee of *Lift Every Voice and Sing II*, giving the book shape and meaning—and I am happy to announce that that hymnal will be dedicated to his blessed memory.

Lastly, Curtis, a man of gentle spirit, who quietly but effectively went about his work, was an inspiration to others, including those aspiring to holy orders (significant in itself in a day when black vocations are woefully few because too many of clergy are too embittered to commend the priesthood to young men and women). And in his last days, those of who were close to him were inspired by his courage. It was courageous Curtis who summoned me to his beside to be his amanuensis and then dictated, with clarity of vision, his wishes and instructions—down to the last rubric—for his own burial. It was a courageous Curtis who told his grandmother that he was not afraid of death but rather was only concerned about his family's sufferings. It was courageous Curtis who, when he knew he was dying, never ceased to be guided by the words of the hymn: "If I can help somebody along the way, then my living shall not be in vain." Although he knew he was dying, he went to North Carolina to preach Monroe Freeman's installation; although he knew he was dying, he went to New York to play for

Bert Gibson's funeral; although he knew he was dying, he came to the black clergy conference last month to coordinate our music and worship. It was courageous Curtis who, earlier this month, after the service at the Church of the Advocate, could say, "It is finished." In dying, Curtis taught us how to live.

All of this does not mean that Curtis was perfect, just a little lower than the angels. Like all of us sinful human beings who have fallen short of the glory of God, there were times when he had done those things that he ought not to have done and left undone those things that he ought to have done. Indeed, his besetting sin was likely the flip-side of his life of service, because the traits of those who take servant ministry seriously, however laudable, often result in a self-denial, a self-negation, a failure to look out for "number one." Virtually boundless concern for others means that one's own problems often get a low priority. So like the Blessed Apostle, desiring "to give no offense in anything" he suffered "afflictions, necessities and distresses . . . tumults and labors, watching and fastings," but also, like Saint Paul, he could say, "By the word of truth, the power of God, by the armor of righteousness on the right and on the left . . . as unknown and yet well known; as sorrowful yet always rejoicing, as poor yet making many rich, as having nothing and yet possessing all things" (2 Cor 6:7–10).

It may well be that, in his earthly pilgrimage, Curtis found comfort and solace in the words of that great hymn:

> When peace like a river attendeth my way,
> When sorrows like sea billows roll;
> Whatever my lot, that hast taught me to say
> It is well, it is well with my soul.

And even when his body was wracked with disease and he lay at the point of death, he could sing:

> Though Satan should buffet, though trials should come,
> Let this blest assurance control;
> That Christ has regarded my helpless estate
> And has shed his own blood for my soul.

And now, Jesus Christ, by the power of the Resurrection, has opened up for Curtis the gates of everlasting life. Curtis has been appointed chief sacristan and assistant organist in those heavenly precincts, "where sorrow and pain are no more, neither sighing, but life everlasting." He has had to cut slits in his voluminous Wippells surplice so that the feathers of his wings will not be ruffled, and he has suggested to the Almighty that the celestial choir, accustomed to signing Mozart's *Coronation Mass* and Bach's *Mass in B Minor*, might also sing Lena McLin's *Eucharist of the Soul*—at least occasionally. And so Curtis, content in the place "where no trouble distractions can bring," can now belt out:

> And Lord, haste the day when the faith shall be sight,
> The clouds be rolled back as a scroll
> The trump shall resound and the Lord shall descend,
> Even so—it is well with my soul.

And the heavenly choir, in chorus with angels and archangels, with prophets, apostles, and martyrs, with the Blessed Virgin Mary, with blessed Luke, Blessed Monica, Blessed Absalom, and all the saints shall take up the refrain:

> It is well—with my soul.
> It is well, it is well, with my soul.

Rest eternal grant unto him, O Lord
And let light perpetual shine upon him.
May his soul and the souls of all the faithful departed
Through the mercy of God, rest in peace and rise in glory.
AMEN.

Poet, Prankster, Paterfamilias

JOSEPH PAUL SCHEETZ (1908–1997)
Preached in Calvary Church, Pittsburgh
12 June 1997

Let not your hearts be troubled. (John 14:1)

WHEN AN EMPLOYER RECEIVES a resume, he or she may well be impressed with the applicant "on paper," as we say, but a hire will not take place until the hopeful employee is met face to face. The employer is interested in the human side of the applicant, not simply the raw data. A newspaper obituary is, as it were, one's final resume. It chronicles the raw data—the milestones—of one's life: birthdate, schools, positions held, club and church affiliations. Today, as we gather to offer thanks to Almighty God for the life and witness of J. Paul Scheetz and commend him to the never-failing providence of a merciful and loving God, we remember those unique qualities of his that made him precious in God's sight.

Paterfamilias Paul was a loving man. His nine nieces and nephews and twenty great-nieces and great-nephews can well bear testimony to that fact. Their affection and admiration of him are genuine (and I use the present tense advisedly) because his love and concern for them were genuine. Each one occupied a special place in his heart. But there is absolutely no question in anyone's mind that Paul's heart belonged to Alice. Their love story is the stuff of which novels are made. It began sometime before that beautiful day fifty-four years ago when they exchanged vows at this altar. It began in this church on the day that Paul saw Alice Rust sitting between her parents, at which time he announced to all within earshot: "That's the one for me!" He then went through the proper channels and arranged to be properly introduced—at a Calvary Church function, of course.

Since their marriage, their home, in the words of the wedding service, has been "a haven of blessing and of peace." I could tell that by the undying affection and devotion in Alice's eyes after Paul's death. The priest knows that some widows are so distraught when planning a funeral that they mumble to the rector between sobs, "Anything you say," or, "Whatever you think best." Not so, Mrs. Paul Scheetz. Alice chose hymns because they had particular meaning for them, and she personally went home, opened her Bible, and read through each of the possible lessons, and chose those that were especially significant—those that spoke to Paul's spirit. No, her last loving gesture for Paul would not be taken lightly; it would not even be left to the liturgical expertise of the rector. Even the title of this service was Alice's decision: "I don't like 'memorial service,'" she said. "I want it to say 'service in thanksgiving for the life of Paul Scheetz.'" Yes, she who, for more than half a century, had lovingly cared for her husband, in sickness and in health, would take this final tribute very seriously.

Prankster Paul was a fun-loving man. His family will long remember his whimsical bowties and his water-squirting boutonniere.

Commander Paul was a patriotic man. Having seen action in both the European and Pacific theatres, he knew well the high price paid for the freedom that we all enjoy and most of us take for granted.

Farmer Paul was an adventuresome man. While those a decade or two younger than the Scheetzes had parked themselves in the nearest rocking chair, the octogenarian Mr. and Mrs. Scheetz decided to raise llamas at their farm.

Uncle Paul was a caring man. While many on their death bed are preoccupied with the state of their own soul, trying desperately to make amends for their life and to set things right with

God at the eleventh hour, Paul Scheetz, who, in the words of one of the great prayers, "having the testimony of a good conscience," spent his final conscious hours inquiring after the well-being of his extended family of which he was the unquestioned patriarch. He seemed to be assuring them, "Let not your hearts be troubled."

Poet Paul was a bright man with a keen intellect, who never ceased to delight those around him. Because he was especially fond of limericks, the preacher begs the indulgence of his family and friends and asks to be exonerated of all charges of irreverence for offering the following in Paul's memory:

> There once was a man named Paul Scheetz,
> Accomplisher of many great feats;
> He approached Miss Rust's father,
> And said "Sir, I'd rather
> Be Alice's, for my heart bleats."
>
> Journalist, poet, and farmer,
> Seldom irate but much calmer;
> Avuncular, witty,
> Displaying great pity
> For every niece, nephew, and llama.
>
> And so Paul, we bid you farewell,
> For if we the truth were to tell,
> We give God the glory
> For the wonderful story
> Your life's been, O servant, done well!

"Not to be served but to serve."

WESLEY WENTZ POSVAR (1925–2001)
Preached in Calvary Church, Pittsburgh
31 July 2001

The Lord has anointed me to bring good tidings to the
afflicted; he has sent me to bind up the broken hearted,
to proclaim liberty to the captives, and the opening of
prison to them that are bound. (Isaiah 61:1)

WE LIVE IN A world of specialists, a world in which people's expertise is often in one narrowly defined area or endeavor. Gone forever are the days of the general practitioner. Physicians are dermatologists or obstetricians. People seem to have a penchant, moreover, for categorizing and pigeonholing each other. Our fellow human beings are either type A or type B. They are, thanks to Meyers and Briggs, E or I, J or P. They are right-brain or left-brain. Wesley Wentz Posvar defied such codification. He possessed characteristics and traits that seldom reside in the same individual. He was a genius who never lost the common touch. He was both an academic and a militarist. He was, as a friend has described him, a fighter pilot trapped in the body of a scholar. But much to the amazement and, at times, the chagrin of his friends and colleagues, Wesley could migrate from the Pentagon to the halls of academe, always making a safe and flawless landing. He could exchange his pilot's headgear and goggles for the professor's mortarboard and spectacles—and not miss a beat. Although Wesley Posvar lived a year and a half into the twenty-first century, he was every inch a Renaissance man!

Because he was a Renaissance man (and not a narrow specialist), he could always see the big picture. This is why he could find the University of Pittsburgh on the brink of receivership and leave it a solvent institution with a multimillion-dollar endowment. This is why a little known regional institution of higher learning could become, under his assiduous leadership, a world class university. Not bound by convention, he could push the envelope, forging relationships between Pitt and universities in Cuba. This is why he could recognize that the university was in the middle of a great city and establish the Center for Social and Urban Research. This is why he had the good sense to woo Mildred Miller, a renowned opera singer, with whom he celebrated the golden anniversary of marriage only a year ago.

So we gather today to give thanks to Almighty God for this man of letters, this man of accomplishments. But, my brothers and sisters, I would like to suggest to you this morning that neither accomplishments nor letters get us into heaven. Degrees and pedigrees are not the admission ticket. Acts of love, expressing concern for others, and making a difference in people's lives are what matters. When Wesley landed his plane on the feathery tarmac of the celestial airport, he could hold his head high in the knowledge that he had reached out to the least, the lost, and the last in society.

He had, in the words of the Prophet Isaiah—words which Jesus himself used in his first sermon as a blueprint for his ministry—"brought good tidings to the afflicted, he had bound up the brokenhearted, and proclaimed liberty to the captives" (Isa 61:1). Wesley could report that he eschewed the idea of the ivory tower and, accordingly, established branch campuses throughout the region. He could point to the community development projects sponsored and maintained by Pitt. He could inform St. Peter that, unlike some of his counterparts in the Sixties and Seventies, he didn't dismiss student demonstrators as upstarts but instead sat on the floor with them, listened to their concerns, and took action on their behalf. The heavenly checklist would have examples of how

Wesley, long before it was fashionable, saw the value to all parties concerned of a multiracial and multicultural society.

Perhaps the kind of man Wesley Posvar was is summed up in a story told to me by an African American member of his faculty. Dr. Posvar was approached for membership in a certain club whose unwritten (yet strictly observed) policy was that it did not admit blacks. He refused to join under such circumstances and proposed to his black colleague that they should be apply for membership together. They would either be admitted together or turned down together. Yet again, Wesley Posvar pushed the envelope; yet again, he flew in the face of convention; yet again, he challenged the mores of a town that, for so long, had missed the boat when it came to race relations. And yet again, Wesley Wentz Posvar prevailed. He was committed, once more in the words of the prophet Isaiah, "to grant to those who mourn in Zion to give them a garland instead of ashes, the oil of gladness instead of mourning, the mantle of praise instead of a faint spirit" (Isa 61:3).

By happy coincidence, today is the feast of Saint Ignatius Loyola, the founder of the Society of Jesus (better known as the Jesuits) and, like our departed brother, a great scholar. But there is a further parallel. At an early age, Ignatius embarked upon a military career, but a series of events led him to give up that vocation. Historians tell us that Ignatius hung up his sword at the altar of the Blessed Virgin Mary and decided to become a soldier for Christ instead. He then found new joy and fulfillment in service to others. When all is said and done, Wesley Wentz Posvar would probably best wish to be remembered not as a Rhodes Scholar, a brigadier general, or a distinguished chancellor of a renowned university; instead, he would want to be remembered as one who, like Ignatius, found joy in service to others, as an agent for social change. It is this legacy, this challenge, that he leaves to his grandsons Wesley, Winston, Nicholas, Christopher, GianMarco, Brian, and Derek, each the apple of his grandfather's eye. We are certain that each of them, in his own way, will rise to this challenge and, in so doing, will honor the memory of their grandfather, who, in the spirit of his Lord, came not to be served, but to serve. AMEN.

"Why?"

JEREMY KIM RUDDY (1972–2003)
Preached in Calvary Church, Pittsburgh
16 April 2003

In my Father's house there are many mansions. (John 14:1)

THE PSALMIST TELLS US that the span of a man's life is threescore years and ten—seventy years—and, if he be especially fortunate, eighty (Ps 90:10). Those figures have been adjusted nowadays, perhaps. A dear friend of mine, a bishop of the church, died last week at seventy, and everybody said he had died young! But no matter what the number is in our minds, when someone dies at an age far short of it, we say that death was premature. We say it was untimely. This has always struck me as playing God. Who are we to say which deaths are timely and which are untimely? To the One we call Eternal, present at the beginning of Creation itself, a year, a decade, and a century are all the same, little more than the twinkling of an eye. I always think that the question we should ask at the time of such a death is not, "How long?" but, "How?" How did that person live his life? How did he touch the lives of people with whom he came into contact? Can that person sing the words of an old hymn, "If I can help somebody along the way, then my living has not been in vain?" Jeremy certainly could have sung such a song. Longevity in and of itself is not a virtue. We know people who, as the saying goes, do little more in the years allotted

87

to them except draw breath and a paycheck. At the time of death, as difficult as may be, we must learn to ask questions about the caliber of a person's life, and not its length. By that standard, we can give thanks to God for Jeremy's example to others, even as we mourn his loss.

This morning, we gather in this church to commit to God's care and providence the soul of our brother departed, Jeremy Kim Ruddy. And while we may well ask this morning the "How?" and the "How long?" questions, if we are honest, the question gnawing at our hearts is "Why?" Why would a man in the prime of life, a man who was the product of a loving family, a man who had found Jennifer, a woman to whom he was devoted and with whom he was looking forward to spending the rest of his life—why would such a man take his own life? What was troubling his soul? What deep dark secret was he harboring in his breast? What demons possessed him? We would like to have answers to these questions. We would like to understand. "Inquiring minds want to know." We would like to wrap up everything like those elegant blue boxes from Tiffany's with the perfectly tied white satin bow. But, the truth of the matter is that, while speculations and theories will abound, we will never really know. And I am afraid that, if you have come to church this morning for the answer to these questions, you will leave disappointed. Church, contrary to common belief, does not provide answers to all of life's questions, but it provides two things that are even better: a community of faith in which we can ask the questions and some guidelines about how to conduct our lives, despite our ignorance and uncertainty. When all is said and done, some practical advice might be more helpful in the long run than simply satisfying our intellectual curiosity. And presumptuous preacher that I am, I will offer you such advice this morning.

First, what we can learn from these tragic circumstances is the importance of being vulnerable. Perhaps, in school, some of you had to memorize William Ernest Henley's poem, *Invictus*. It contains the words,

> It matters not how strait the gate,
> How charged with punishments the scroll,

I am the master of my fate:

I am the captain of my soul.[11]

Now this may be good poetry, but it is lousy theology. We
are *not* ultimately in charge of our lives. Sometimes, with all due
respects to Mr. Henley, we *are* afraid, we *do* wince, we *do* cry aloud.
We are not supermen and superwomen. We are dependent upon
one another. And the great paradox of life, as we learn from Jesus
himself, is that we best exhibit our strength when we show our
weakness.

Second, we must learn to trust. When we are able to trust
someone, it means that we do not have to bear the cross alone.
Trusting is admittedly risky, but it is essential to us to have trust-
worthy fellow pilgrims along the way.

And most important, we must learn not to lose heart. We
stand in the midst of Holy Week, with the Cross looming over
us. But we know that Good Friday—our sufferings, our trials and
tribulations—does not constitute the final answer. The joy of Resurrection morning is within our grasp.

I spoke to my mother yesterday and told her that I had a funeral today, the funeral of a young man who had taken his own life.
She said, "Harold, how will you handle that?" I said, "I don't know,
Mother, I'm praying about what I will say." But as the conversation
continued, I realized that my mother, dyed-in-the-wool Episcopalian that she is, was not asking a homiletical question, but a liturgical one. She was not asking how I would preach the sermon, but
how I would conduct the service itself. Her memory of a funeral,
long decades ago, of one who had taken his own life, was seared
in her mind. She related to me that the body came through the
west doors of the church, into the narthex, and it stayed there. It
remained at the entrance to the church! It did not come down the
aisle. It did not approach the altar. That was the distinction made
in some places in those days. A church which preached that "there
is a wideness in God's mercy," a church which declares absolution

11. Henley, *Invictus.*

to penitent sinners, nonetheless declared suicide the unforgivable sin. The church just didn't get it!

Obviously, the church had not read this morning's Gospel. Jesus tells us: "In my Father's house there are many rooms." What he is saying is that there is a place reserved for each and every one of us, regardless of our race, gender, nationality, sexual orientation, or the circumstances of our death. We do not know what led to Jeremy's death, but we know for a certainty that God has opened up for him the gates of everlasting life, and that one of those rooms, behind the Pearly Gates, has Jeremy's name on it—and that should give us some comfort.

There is an old Negro spiritual based on this text; perhaps you've heard it: "Plenty good room, plenty good room, plenty good room in my Master's kingdom." And Negro spirituals, lest we forget, aren't just nice songs, they are liberation theology set to music. The barefoot slave could sing of a heaven where "all God's children got shoes." The slave, deprived of hearth and home, could sing of a heaven where there's "plenty good room."

"In my father's house, there are many rooms," we read in Saint John's Gospel. This verse might have special significance for Jeremy. Perhaps more than most, he was searching for his room, his place, his niche. The family made up of Geraldine, Frank, Jeremy, Mark, Matthew, and Jennifer looked like the United Nations. They remind me of a song I learned in Sunday School:

> Red and yellow, black and white, they are precious in his sight,
> Jesus loves the little children of the world.

But this outward and visible sign of racial harmony was not everybody's cup of tea. It could even be threatening to people who instinctively bond only with their tribe, race, or clan. And perhaps Jeremy was caught in the middle. Perhaps he was the most stung by the insensitivity, the unkind remarks, and the racism, overt and covert. But we shall never really know.

What we do know is this: Jesus assures us, "Let not your hearts be troubled. In my father's house there are many rooms. If it were not so, I would have told you. I go to prepare a place for you" (John 14:1–2). Jesus is talking about a place where we are all guests—A-list guests at his heavenly banquet, a place where the walls that we erect, the distinctions that we make, the pecking orders that we invent here on earth are unheard of. A place where fear is unknown. A place, in the words of a great hymn, "Where no troubles distraction can bring." This is the place, my sisters and brothers in Christ, where Jeremy has found his niche, his room, his home at last, in the arms of a loving, compassionate God who welcomes him unconditionally.

May his soul, no longer tested, no longer troubled, no longer tortured, rest in peace. AMEN.

"For the joy of human love, brother, sister, parent, child."

CHARLES COVERT ARENSBERG (1913–2011)
Preached in Calvary Church, Pittsburgh
13 July 2001

> The Lord is good to those who wait for him, to the soul
> that seeks him. It is good that one should wait quietly for
> the salvation of the Lord. (Lam 3:26–27)

A FEW MONTHS AFTER arriving at Calvary five years ago, I was invited to be the preacher at Thursday morning chapel at St. Edmund's Academy. As I was waiting to join the procession, a first-grade girl craned her neck to look up at my towering frame and announced: "I know you. You go to my church!" This out-of-the-mouths-of-babes comment humbled me. It served to remind me that I had stepped into the history of a parish that had flourished for 140 years before my arrival and will likely flourish for just as long after my departure. Entering *in medias res*, as it were, I have met people at various stages in their spiritual journeys. I met Charley Arensberg when he was well into his sunset years, and my first prolonged memory of him was at a luncheon he hosted last year for his many friends in Pittsburgh. Though in frail health, he was ever the gracious host, making pleasantries, reminiscing with colleagues, and accepting the accolades of his admirers. Like Calvary Church, Charley had flourished long before I got here, and now that he has departed this life and is in the nearer presence

of his Maker, he will flourish long after I leave. Today, we pause
to give thanks for Charley's life, as we commit him to the never-
failing care and mercy of Almighty God. And to assist us in this
task, I ask that you meditate with me on these words from the
Lamentations of Jeremiah:

> The Lord is good to those who wait for him, to the soul
> that seeks him. It is good that one should wait quietly for
> the salvation of the Lord. (Lam 3:26–27)

Charley was one of a rare breed of human beings—now almost entirely extinct in this "it's all about me" generation—who
wait upon God, who quietly seek his salvation. Charley quietly
went about his life and his work, without desire for fanfare or adu-
lation. His favorite time to come to church was Good Friday—not
because he was morbid and didn't recognize the power of the Resurrection in his life. No, Charley was one who quietly went about
the business of righting wrongs through the law, his friendships,
and his actions, and, for that reason, perhaps, he identified with the
Crucified Savior, who went about the business of righting wrongs
through his Death on the Cross. Or perhaps it is because Charley,
who always gave of himself, identified with the pain of others.

Charley was a preservationist. A great history buff (who even
delighted in giving history quizzes—complete with prizes—to his
young children and their classmates), he loved and developed an
appreciation for old buildings long before his fellow Pittsburghers
caught on that their city had anything worth preserving. His interests led him to help found the Pittsburgh History & Landmarks
Foundation, which he was to chair for thirty years.

But Charley didn't believe everything was worth preserving.
At the height of the Civil Rights movement, he fought tooth and
nail against those who wished to preserve the institution of racism.
Risking life and limb, he joined other young attorneys in the Mississippi delta as a volunteer for the Lawyers' Constitutional Defense Committee. A man accustomed to standing in the way of the
wrecking ball, on this occasion, Charley deftly wielded it, attacking
what was to some a sacred structure built upon the presumption

of white entitlement. A man accustomed to riding to the hounds, Charley found himself riding herd on white supremacists who moved heaven and earth to prevent blacks from voting. A man accustomed to representing the interests of Pittsburgh's first families, Charley found himself defending poor black activists in their struggle to claim their birthright to life, liberty, and the pursuit of happiness. Why did Charley do this? Because he felt that this is where the Lord had called him to go. Like Jeremiah, he believed he had been sent "to pluck up and to break down, to destroy and to overthrow, to build and to plant" (Jer 1:10).

Despite his accomplishments and achievements, Charley probably wanted to be remembered most as one utterly devoted to his family. In an era of "trophy" spouses and children, family members who are trotted out to provide an automatic stamp of respectability, Charley loved and was in love with his family. He adored Gay, his wife of fifty-five years, his brothers, his children, and his grandchildren. Long before "how-to" books on the subject flooded the market, his own prescription for effective parenting was simple: "Shield your disappointments, celebrate your children, and simply love them." Charley could well have written the words of the hymn we have just sung:

> For the joy of human love, brother, sister, parent, child,
> Friends on earth, and friends above, for all gentle thoughts and mild.

In today's Gospel, Jesus tells of the reward that he has in store for those who have patiently waited upon him: "In my Father's house there are many mansions," he tells us, "And when I go and prepare a place for you, I will come again and will take you to myself that where I am you may be also" (John 14:2–3). If there is any justice at all, Charley has already been conveyed to heaven in a specially fitted car from the Duquesne Incline and has found that his celestial digs bear a striking resemblance to Mr. Richardson's Romanesque Courthouse. But regardless of the nature of his heavenly appointments, we know that there is a special place there for a man whose legacy to his family, his church, his community, and his nation has been so rich.

In the Arensberg household, the family say goodnight to each other and their children with this wish: "God guard you and keep you through the night." Today, we say to Charley, "May the God who has guarded and kept you every night of your earthly life, now guard and keep you through all eternity." AMEN.

"Son of Encouragement."

DWIGHT LYNN WHITE (1949–2008)
Preached in Calvary Church, Pittsburgh
11 June 2008

Let not your hearts be troubled. (John 14:1)

IF WE WERE HONEST with ourselves at this moment, we would have to admit to a whole range of emotions. We are incredulous that Dwight has been taken so suddenly from our midst. We are shocked at the thought that he is no longer in our circle. We are saddened that all of us, especially his family, are bereft of his comforting and reassuring presence. And we may be angry—even angry at God—for allowing this to happen.

If we can identify with any or all of these emotions, it may be because, in our limited vocabulary of faith, we human beings are often only able to describe death in one of two ways. Somewhere in the back of our minds is the Psalmist's declaration that a lifespan should be threescore years and ten (or, if we are lucky, fourscore), so we declare that the deaths of people who die in their seventies and eighties to be timely, but those who fall short of that biblical standard we declare as untimely. So we play God and, in our arrogance, refer to Dwight's death as untimely. "He was too young to die," we say. "He had so much more to offer." "He was in his prime." "His work wasn't done."

This afternoon, I would ask that we reexamine our conventional wisdom. In the first place, in the eyes of God, who reckons existence in eternities and not decades, the difference between fifty-eight and, say, eighty-eight is infinitesimal. Listen to the words of Isaac Watts's great hymn: "A thousand ages in thy sight are like an evening gone/short as the watch that ends the night, before the rising sun."[12] If that reasoning doesn't grab you, try this: Instead of zeroing in on the quantity of life, giving people credit for longevity—or, as a friend of mine put it, drawing breath and a paycheck—let us learn instead to concentrate on the quality of life and give people credit for what they were able to accomplish, despite the limited time allotted to them. At life's end, each of us should be able to say, "If I have helped somebody along the way, then my living has not been in vain." Whose lives have we touched? What difference have we made? Is the planet a better place because we have trod on its surface? Jesus, it will be remembered, walked this earth for a mere thirty-three years. Martin Luther King was felled by a sniper's bullet nine months shy of his fortieth birthday. The prolific composer Wolfgang Amadeus Mozart died at thirty-five. By this measure, Dwight's life was long and rich.

But the fact remains that we are never really ready for death, no matter when or how it comes. Even a protracted illness does not prepare us, does not absorb the shock. The transition from life to death seems so final, so irrevocable. So when death comes, we often rely on words. As we gather to give thanks today for Dwight's life, we are comforted by the words of Jesus, "Let not your hearts be troubled." Jesus uses these words as he speaks to his disciples in a moment of crisis. Gathered together in the Upper Room, he tells them that he will be departing from them, but he tells them not to worry. The disciples didn't know or understand where he would be going, and it was not at all certain if they could go with him, but he tells them not to worry. Everything seemed to be on the verge of collapse. One of Jesus' disciples would betray him; and Peter, his right hand man, would deny him, but Jesus told them not to worry, not to fear, and not to fret. Jesus was warning them of the type of fear that leads to paralysis, that sets in when we worry so much we are unable to function. I think this verse is especially appropriate

12. Watts, "O God Our Help."

this morning because we can hear Dwight mouthing these words. Dwight did not let his heart be troubled; he took things in stride. He gave new definition to being laid back. And we do well to emulate his example.

Today, in the church's calendar, it happens to be the feast of Saint Barnabas. His real name was Joseph, but his fellow apostles gave him the name Barnabas, which means, "Son of encouragement." Barnabas was the go-getter, the doer, the pacesetter, and the risk-taker. He was the apostle who encouraged his fellow disciples and spurred them on in the face of adversity. Dwight White has been our own apostle of encouragement. His teammates can attest to his encouragement on the field, but Dwight didn't stop encouraging people when he hung up his jersey. For young people, he became a role model without peer. He gave of himself unstintingly. It can never be said of Dwight White that he didn't give back to the community that produced him, and beyond. Goodwill Industries, the Salvation Army, the Boy Scouts of America, and the PACE School are just some of the charities he supported. And because Karen has asked that donations in Dwight's memory be given to the August Wilson Center, of which they have been staunch supporters and fund-raisers, I want you to know that I was sorely tempted to break with Episcopal decorum and tradition, to pass the plate at this service, and to send the money to Neil Barclay! But cooler heads prevailed.

Dwight was no pie-eyed visionary or Lady Bountiful-type do-gooder. He was a consummate politician in the best sense of the word. He wielded power, rubbed shoulders with the powerful, even as he spoke the truth to power. He had the privilege, with some of his fellow Steelers, of riding on Barack Obama's campaign bus, and he took great pride in telling me, when I visited him in the hospital, that he had been elected to be a delegate to the Democratic National Convention this summer. Now I am just a simple parson, who professes little knowledge of matters political (except what I've managed to pick up along the way in the Episcopal Church), and I don't know how these things work. But we are honored today to have the Governor, the County Executive, and the Mayor in this hallowed place, giving thanks for the life of Dwight White. Couldn't these gentlemen have a little caucus over punch and figure out a way that Mrs. Dwight White could take her late husband's seat in Denver? Just a thought.

After a mere twelve years in this city, I am a Pittsburgher only by adoption and grace, so I never knew Dwight White as the Mad Dog. It was not my privilege to hang out with him when he was part of that virtually impenetrable defense known as the Steel Curtain. I was not acquainted with the living legend who left his hospital bed, stricken with pneumonia, to lead a successful charge against the Minnesota Vikings. I arrived on the scene too late to rejoice with Dwight in those glory days when he helped the Steelers clinch four Super Bowl victories.

But I am proud to have known Dwight White as a friend, a confidant, a fraternity brother, someone to chew the fat with or have a drink with. It was a privilege to know him as Karen's loving and devoted husband, and yes, as the doting and indulgent father to Stacey, the apple of his eye. That said, the greatest privilege I experienced in the course of our friendship was to function as his pastor. During those hospital visits, we prayed together, we laughed together, and we cried together. I listened to him when he said, "This is serious, H." On his last day, I was able to anoint him, commending him to the never-failing care of a merciful Savior. And finally, there was that holiest of moments, as the family and I gathered round his bed, praying, reading psalms, and saying our goodbyes as he breathed his last.

My favorite memory of Dwight dates back to the summer of 2004, when ten of us decided to spend a week together in a chateau in the south of France. It was all we could do to convince Dwight to go. For someone to whom "roughing it" means staying in a four-star hotel, the idea of a drafty sixteenth-century chateau was a hard sell. And we won't even mention the 150-Euro taxi ride from the airport, about which Dwight complained bitterly for at least two years. Dwight's French was minimal, but he communicated just fine with his winning personality, charisma, and charm. After a few days of gourmet dining, Dwight decided that we would forego pate, escargots, pommes frites and other French delicacies, and would instead have a down-home Texas barbecue. He descended on the market in beautiful downtown Mirepoix, where, larger than life, he wowed his newly-adopted French neighbors, to whom he soon became known as "le grand Texan." He went from boucherie to boucherie and managed to buy up every last spare rib in town. Then he brought them back to the chateau, whipped up his secret sauce, and grilled the ribs on the terrace. They were smokin'! We sat down to a soul food dinner in the middle of France, thanks to Dwight, who, consummate ambassador that he was, always managed to leave his mark, his influence, and his unique stamp wherever he went.

All of us are enriched for having known him, loved him, and having been embraced by him, literally and figuratively. (Any recipient of his bear hug knew at once why he was part of something called the Steel Curtain!) The prayer for Saint Barnabas says that that apostle sought not his own renown but instead gave to the support of others. This was Dwight—the trash-talking, self-deprecating, fun-loving man who, behind his eighth of a ton frame, was an affectionate, loving, gentle, and humble individual, a man who, although he usually towered over everybody else in the room, never lost the common touch. This is the Dwight White for whom our Lord Jesus Christ has prepared a place. This is the man for whom Jesus has said, "In my father's house are many rooms"—although I am sure Dwight, who always went first class, would prefer the translation "many mansions."

May he rest in peace. AMEN.

"An officer and a Christian gentleman."

GUY MARTIN NEWLAND (1928–2008)
Preached in Calvary Church, Pittsburgh
20 June 2008

Let not your hearts be troubled. (John 14:1)

THE STORY IS TOLD about an old priest who believed very strongly in the practice of sacramental confession. He was of the opinion that each practicing Christian should go to the "box" early and often. As a result, Father Smith never missed the opportunity to talk about confession and preach about confession. No matter the season—Lent, Easter, Advent, Christmas—the message was the same: make your confession. Finally, the parish council got together and decided to send a delegation to the rectory. They assured their pastor that they did indeed avail themselves of the sacrament of Penance and there was no need to preach about it at every mass. Father Smith got the message. He agreed, and seemed to show signs of reform for a week or two, but when the Feast of Saint Joseph came around, he got into the pulpit, and said, "Today is Saint Joseph's Day. Saint Joseph was a carpenter, and in his life he must have made a few confessionals, which reminds me . . ."

Guy Newland was a lover of things Castillian. His roots in Panama and his time spent in such places as Mexico and Spain created in him a love of Spanish culture and history, and so, like Father Smith's parishioners, who were always treated to pronouncements on his favorite topic, those of us who enjoyed Guy's company could always expect to be regaled with stories about Montezuma, Generalisimo Franco, or the Panama Canal—even if the conversation were about knitting or Eskimos! When I told Guy that my grandfather left Barbados to work on the Panama Canal, he told me that this fact would make it possible for me to obtain Panamanian citizenship! His stories about such matters always punctuated his remarks at the Junta, a club of some thirty gentlemen who meet once or twice a month (in black tie, of course) to listen to papers written by its members. I shall always be grateful to Guy for the confidence he showed in me by nominating me for membership!

Proud of his military service, Guy was a patriot in the best sense of that word. Unfortunately, that word is now too often tinged with suggestions of fanaticism, intolerance, and even bigotry, epitomized by the America-love-it-or-leave-it crowd. Not so with Guy. He believed in the ideals for which this country stands and for the sacrifices that had been made by many in the preservation of those ideals. When, during a recent visit, he noticed my Obama pin, we talked a little about the political climate and what each candidate had to offer. At the end of the conversation, Guy simply said, "Well I'll be voting for McCain—he's a Navy man, after all."

Guy was one of the few people of whom it can be said that he was a scholar and a gentleman. But we would have to qualify that description by saying that he was a scholar and a *Christian* gentleman. He was a proud alumnus of the Kent School and of Princeton. It was at Kent School that the Holy Cross fathers grounded him in the faith that would sustain him for the nearly eight decades of his life—and where, like the fictional Father Smith, real priests urged him to go to confession. That faith saw him through his world travels, his military service, his professional career, and, above all, his life as a husband and father. Guy was never far from the church, no matter the part of the world in which he found himself. Here, at Calvary, he was very proud to be a lay reader and chalice bearer, and he especially liked to serve at the noon mass on Sundays, in the Lady Chapel. And how well I remember how sad

I was to receive a note from Guy a few years ago, saying that he would have to give up that ministry he cherished so much, since he was getting just a little wobbly. It seems altogether fitting and proper that, in a few moments, we will commit his mortal remains to a place just a few feet from the altar where he was privileged to administer communion.

Today's Gospel lesson begins with the familiar words, "Let not your hearts be troubled." Jesus uses these words as he speaks to his disciples in a moment of crisis. Gathered together in the Upper Room, he tells them that he will be departing from them, but he tells them not to worry. The disciples didn't know or understand where he would be going, and it was not at all certain if they could go with him, but he tells them not to worry. Everything seemed to be on the verge of collapse. One of Jesus' disciples would betray him; and Peter, his right hand man, would deny him, but Jesus told them not to worry, not to fear, and not to fret. Jesus was warning them of the type of fear that leads to paralysis, that sets in when we worry so much we are unable to function. This morning, these words offer comfort to all of us who now find ourselves bereft of Guy's presence, Guy's company, Guy's companionship. But they are fitting for another reason—that is, that we can hear Guy saying these words, for he was a man not easily troubled, not easily upset. He seemed to me, at least, to be unflappable. He would be the first to tell us not to fret about his death, not to worry about him who now resides in one of those many mansions that Jesus promised he would provide. He would tell us, too, in the same breath, that we should give thanks for those special moments we were able to spend together and to be sustained by those memories.

Three days ago, I was summoned to the hospital, where, with Joan and other members of the family, we gathered round Guy just after he had breathed his last. We recited the Litany and commended Guy to the merciful care of his Savior. But what I remember most about that intimate gathering were Joan's words. She said she didn't know what she would do without him. She looked forward to every morning, when Guy got up first, and set the table for breakfast. And when they were at breakfast, it was Guy who encouraged Joan to eat more heartily, to get the day off to a good start. This came across as a little parable—and I remember from Confirmation class that a parable is an earthly story with a heavenly meaning—which depicted Guy Martin Newland not as a dashing officer, a businessman, not as an expert on matters Castillian or as a diplomat, but as a loving, caring man. This is the person whom we commend to the never failing care of Jesus, the Bishop and Shepherd of our souls. AMEN.

"Write the vision. Make it plain upon the tablets."

JOHN GILBERT CRAIG JR. (1933–2010)
Preached in Calvary Church, Pittsburgh
5 June 2010

> Oh that my words were written! Oh that they were in-
> scribed in a book! Oh that with an iron pen and lead they
> were graven in the rock for ever! (Job 19:23–24)

THE PREACHER WHO MUST use words to honor the memory of John Gilbert Craig Jr. faces a daunting task indeed. For John was a lover of words. If we look up "wordsmith" in the dictionary, we would find that Mr. Webster has supplied us with a photograph of John Craig as part and parcel of the definition. We live, as we needn't be reminded, in a world in which Shakespeare's tongue has been reduced to bastardized hieroglyphics by those who tweet, text, and insist that "friend" can be a verb. In the face of these egregious assaults on the language, John Craig stood resolutely on those venerable foundations of prose known as subject and predicate and eschewed with a vengeance such grammatical aberrations as the split infinitive, the dangling participle, and the sentence ending in a preposition. So even as we speak, we can well imagine John, happily ensconced in that neighborhood behind the Pearly Gates reserved for journalists—yes, there *is* such a place—blue pencil in hand, ready to critique this homiletic offering. I take no small comfort, however, in the knowledge that seven years ago, John gave a favorable review in his columns to a sermon I preached at the marriage of his daughter Lindsay.

But John Craig was no mere linguistic purist, a slave to the *Chicago Manual of Style*. John, as the distinguished and beloved editor-in-chief of the *Pittsburgh Post-Gazette*, actually had something to say! And more often than not, he said it unabashedly, letting the proverbial chips fall where they may. A Pittsburgher by adoption and grace, he perched himself, as it were, on the cliffs of Mount Washington and, like a one-man Greek chorus, delivered an ongoing commentary on the drama being acted out below. Believing that the city's problems were "almost entirely attitudinal and self-inflicted," he did not hesitate to criticize the 'Burgh for its insularity and lack of vision, its "timidity and parochialism," or for the level of pretension that accompanied them. While others avoided the topic of race like the plague, John fearlessly drew the parallels between racial discrimination and unemployment, even going so far as to suggest that the poverty level of racial minorities of this city was, to some extent, a consequence of the attention given to the "economics of professional sports." Now John was not incapable of praise for Pittsburgh, but it was often faint at best, as when he suggested that the last two years might eventually be looked upon as the tipping point, "a time when we finally got four decades of negative history behind us."

Not everybody could have gotten away with this, but John was able to. First, he got away with it because it was clear to all and sundry—even to his detractors (and there were a few!)—that John spoke out of a clear sense of conviction. It was clear that he spoke and wrote from his heart, and that he was not merely taking pot shots at this or that sector of the community. Second, John's intellect was such that even those who disagreed with his opinions could not assail the intellectual process that led to them. But John's effectiveness as a communicator had a lot to do with his wit and humor. Using both to good effect, he could disarm his audience. A bitter pill always goes down better with a smile. But what is more, his humor was self-deprecating. When all was said and done, there was a sense in which John did not take himself too seriously. I think he took a page from the book of Dame Margot Fonteyn (I hope John will excuse me for comparing him to a ballerina) who said that when she took the dance seriously, she could perform flawlessly, but if she ever took herself seriously, she'd fall flat on her face!

I had the privilege of spending some time with John on the day before he died. But I want to assure you that this was no ordinary deathbed visitation. John was lucid, intelligible, witty, and humorous, still at the top of his game, even if within hours of his final demise. Let me tell you what I did not see on that Tuesday afternoon. I saw nary a trace of fear. John was able to face—even embrace—his departure from this life as the inevitable end result of his earthly existence. Nor was there any complaining or railing in God's face. No chorus of "Why me?" Instead, John gave thanks for his life. He talked about growing up with his late sister. He talked about his beloved Candace and his children and grandchildren. Then, he invited me to look through the French doors of his bedroom, onto the terrace, and at the shrubbery and trees beyond. "Does it get any more beautiful than this?" he asked. He then recited the Lord's Prayer with conviction and received communion for the last time with thankfulness. He then summed up his life with a rather unorthodox but certainly Craig-esque expression of gratitude: "It's been a helluva ride!" In dying, John taught us how to live. And this is why I read to him the words that the Apostle Paul recited as he faced his death, words found in today's epistle: "I have fought the good fight, I have finished the race, I have kept the faith" (2 Tim 4:7).

The lesson from the Hebrew Scriptures this afternoon is from the book of Job, a man who has long been held up as the quintessential exemplar of patience, suffering, and perseverance. Stripped of his wealth and prosperity, it was Satan's expectation that Job would curse God, but he never does. In fact, he comes to a new and deeper understanding of salvation. It is he who proclaims, in fact, the words immortalized by Mr. Handel: "I know that my redeemer liveth." But before reciting these words, he offers a lament: "Oh that my words were written! Oh that they were inscribed in a book! Oh that with an iron pen and lead they were graven in the rock forever" (Job 19:23–24). In other words, despairing of justice from his friends in his lifetime, Job wishes his words could be persevered imperishably to posterity. In this regard, John Craig has an advantage over Job. John's words have been written; they have been inscribed in many books. Indeed, they are etched in the memories of those whose privilege it was to read them.

My friends, we have come this afternoon to commit to God's never-failing love and mercy not merely a writer, journalist, or a real-life version of Perry White. No, I would like to suggest to you that we come to bury a prophet. Now a prophet is not, as is commonly believed, someone who predicts the future. Rather he is one who interprets—indeed who is called to interpret—the signs of the times for the people. He issues words of warning, he challenges the status quo, he is a champion of the oppressed, and he is a builder of community. The prophet is a risk-taker, sometimes a revolutionary, and always a seeker of justice. And so it was with John. So with this in mind, perhaps his new heavenly neighbors are not Horace Greeley and William Randolph Hearst, but fellow prophets like Amos, who wrote "Let justice roll down like waters, and righteousness like an overflowing stream" (Amos 5:24), or Habakkuk, who said, "Write the vision, make it plain upon the tablets, so that even a runner may read it" (Hab 2:2). But I think John's favorite neighbor is the prophet Ezekiel, who wrote, "Whether they hear or refuse to hear, they will know that there has been a prophet among them" (Ezek 2:5). AMEN.

"To do justice, love kindness, and walk humbly with your God."

MILTON AMIGER WASHINGTON (1935–2016)
Preached in Calvary Church, Pittsburgh
27 October 2016

> Our eyes are fixed, not on the things that are seen, but on
> the things that are unseen; for what is seen passes away;
> what is unseen is eternal. (2 Cor 4:18)

JUST A FEW SHORT weeks ago, Milton, Nancy, and I sat in their living room and discussed what too many people never get around to discussing—funeral arrangements. Although Milt's heath seemed to have rebounded, we knew that the overall situation was that his condition was tenuous at best. Unlike some who would find the topic uncomfortable or even distasteful, Milton participated fully in a matter-of-fact kind of way, voicing preferences, for example, as to hymns and lessons. But when we began to talk about the deeper, more spiritual aspects of the service, Mickey said, "Just whip up something suitable for a lukewarm Episcopalian."

Now in the twenty years that I have had the privilege of knowing Milton Amiger Washington, I don't remember ever having the need to contradict him, but I did on this occasion. I told him in no uncertain terms that there was nothing lukewarm about his religion, and that he was a man of deep faith. I didn't fully explain my remarks at that time, but I will do so now that I have a captive audience!

Some people beat up on themselves, believing that being religious means knowing the precise day and time that you were saved; citing chapter and verse for every conceivable occasion; and wearing and referring to a "what would Jesus do" bracelet to settle every religious conundrum. But guess what. The Bible doesn't support such a view. Rather, Micah tells us that religion is summed up in this way: "To do justice, love kindness, and walk humbly with your God" (Mic 6:8). Jesus places emphasis on our inner thoughts and motivation, warning us against doing as the hypocrites do, disfiguring our faces, so that everybody knows that we are fasting (Matt 6:16). The apostle James tells us that, "Pure religion undefiled is to visit the widows and orphans in their affliction and to keep oneself unspotted from the world," (Jas 1:27) and then he drives home the point by reminding us that "faith without works is dead" (Jas 2:17).

Milton Washington understood this. He was self-deprecating. Although the quintessential businessman, dedicated to his work, he didn't take himself too seriously. In fact, we could call him a party animal! In this way, Milt had something in common with Dame Margot Fonteyn, who said that as long as she took the dance seriously, she could perform with grace, but the minute she took herself seriously, she would fall flat on her face! (Only in death would I dare compare Milton Washington to a ballerina!)

Milton was also gracious. He was always the consummate (and well turned out) host. Last Monday, discovering that various out-of-town friends were converging on Pittsburgh, he brought them together with some of us locals over dinner at the Duquesne Club. But he was no less gracious to strangers. With an affectionate hug or a kiss on the cheek, he called guys "buddy" and the ladies "dear," and only his family knew the reason he used those terms of endearment was that he couldn't always remember people's names!

But above all, Mickey was generous. Indeed, his obituary in the *Post-Gazette* referred to him as a philanthropist. He would probably be embarrassed by that term, unless we reminded him that the word really means "lover of humankind." His gifts were first and foremost an expression of love—the kind of love the

Greeks called *agape*—wanting the very best for his fellow human beings, whether they were his employees, the residents for whom he provided affordable housing, or the students whom he enabled to pursue higher education We are all aware of his munificence on behalf of education, the arts, and of this very parish. There are countless individuals who have also benefited from Mickey's largesse—and in all these cases, Mr. Washington sought neither recognition, nor fame, nor glory. His generosity knew no bounds. Nancy even tells the story of how after watching an infomercial about abused animals, he just sat down and wrote a check!

But of course, the lion's share of his love was claimed by his family. How well I remember the Washingtons' golden wedding anniversary six years ago. Mickey, resplendent in a white dinner jacket, beaming from ear to ear, looking into Nancy's eyes as they renewed their vows. Linda and Lara report that, in the parental department, their dad was the "good cop," and Nancy the "bad cop," except for those occasions on which the good cop was informed of his daughters' transgressions, when he could, in a heartbeat, become the bad cop's surrogate! And there were some loving moments remembered, such as the time when Mickey had just dropped Linda off at Harvard, looked up, and, seeing her in the window, just burst into tears. Lara remembers her father teaching her to swim on Martha's Vineyard in the summer of 1976. She remembers the year well because that was also the summer that "Jaws" was released.

What I have to say now is intended for Cecee, Zoe, Kendall, and Tanner, but the rest of you may eavesdrop it you like. First, I want you guys to thank God for the gift of your grandfather—that you were able to benefit from his warm presence, his unbridled devotion, his assiduous attention, and his constant affection that he lavished on you for so many years. Secondly, be sure to imitate the example he has set for you, an example of service, selflessness, and sacrifice. Lastly, it is my prayer that you honor his legacy and not squander it. But by legacy, I don't mean stuff like real estate and bank accounts. I mean intangible things. Today's lesson was chosen for a reason. Saint Paul tells us: "Our eyes are fixed, not on the things that are seen, but on the things that are unseen, for what is seen passes away; what is unseen is eternal" (2 Cor 4:18). Saint Paul is writing to the church at Corinth, a large, bustling city five times as large as Athens. Consumed by their wealth and success, the Corinthians lost their bearings and lost sight of "unseen things," the intangible values that mark us as children of God. Some of those unseen things are honor, integrity, and humility. I have every confidence that you, as you honor your grandfather's memory, will never lose sight of these things, and that the same God who has given you the will to do these things will give you the grace and power to perform them.

My sisters and brothers in Christ, Milton Washington can now, with Saint Paul, proclaim, "I have finished the course, I have fought the fight, I have kept the faith" (2 Tim 4:7). May all of us who have been touched by Milton's appreciation for those aspects of life that truly matter, those of us who have been beneficiaries of his generosity of spirit and his lovingkindness, those of us who have been inspired by Milt's faith, steadfastness, humility, courage, and perseverance now pause and say with King David: "Do you not know that a prince and a great man has this day fallen in Israel?" (2 Sam 3:38).

Rest eternal grant unto Milton, O Lord, and may light perpetual shine upon him. May his soul and the souls of all the faithful, departed through the mercy of God, rest in peace and rise in glory. AMEN.

"It's the spouting whale that gets harpooned."

HENRY LEA HILLMAN (1918–2017)
Preached in Calvary Church, Pittsburgh
21 April 2017

But we know that when Christ appears, we shall be like
him, or we shall him like he is. (1 John 3:2)

THE OBITUARIES ARE UNANIMOUS. The adverbs describing how
Henry carried out his mission and, yes, his ministry in this city
bear a striking resemblance to one another. Mr. Hillman, we are
told, "quietly gave of his time and money." We are informed else-
where that Mr. Hillman "reluctantly attached his name to major
projects he funded." And another comment sums it up: "Mr.
Hillman seemed to live his life privately"—and, if I may add an
adverb of my own, humbly. Despite the power and influence that
Henry wielded, there was no fanfare, no folderol, no bluster, no
braggadocio, and nary a whiff of arrogance or self-importance.
Believing that it's the spouting whale that gets harpooned, Henry
never fell into the trap of which Saint Paul warned the Corinthians,
never thinking of himself more highly than he ought to.

This is because Henry relied on an inner confidence and
sense of self-worth, and the fact that he knew who he was and
Whose he was. I would like to believe that this might be because,
in the providence of Almighty God, Henry Lea Hillman was born
on Christmas Day and died on Good Friday. That does not mean

that Henry was Jesus' alter ego. After all, Henry did not found a church, institute the sacraments, or go about the highways and byways performing miracles (although it can be argued that he did a lot to heal the sick). Rather, I am suggesting that Henry was imbued by his Maker with what one hymn calls "Christlike graces." For like our Lord, he was compassionate, empathetic, and selfless. Unlike some so-called philanthropists who are little more than ATMs with a pulse, Henry understood fully that the philanthropist is, first and foremost, a lover of humankind. And it was Henry's undying love for this community and its citizens that motivated every expression of his indefatigable generosity, whether in the form of a cancer center or a skating rink.

But love, which the Romans called *caritas*, begins at home. And to understand Henry as a loving man, we need only look at his seventy-year love affair with Elsie, a marriage whose success, he explained, was grounded on mutual respect, tolerance, and understanding. When he said, as he often did, that the best thing he ever did was to marry Elsie Hilliard, he meant it. And when he added, "Saying 'Yes, dear,' a lot didn't hurt either," he meant that too. On those occasions that I visited Elsie in the hospital, Henry was often there reading to her, playing gin rummy with her, or just holding her hand, keeping vigil. It was love in action. And this love has cascaded down and embraced three more generations of the Hillman clan, who, today, to borrow a phrase from the book of Proverbs, rise up and call Henry blessed.

Much more could be said about Henry Hillman. He was personable. He could relate, to use a phrase from the old Prayer Book, to "all sorts and conditions" of men and women. Heads of state, CEOs, messenger boys, and clerks were all beneficiaries of Henry's respect and admiration. It was Henry that Kipling had in mind when he wrote: "If you can 'walk with crowds and keep your virtue/Or walk with kings nor lose the common touch.'"[13]

Henry was pragmatic. How well I remember the day when I called on him and Elsie and was ushered into their private dining room atop the Grant Building. I was laden with blueprints for

13. Kipling, "If," 171.

the restoration of the parish house for which the Hillmans had promised to make a lead gift. The plans were admittedly elaborate, with a price tag to match. The only things missing were a pair of turrets and a moat! Henry gave me some advice: "Harold, I've been involved in a few building projects in my day, and I have learned that if you tell the architect how much you have to spend, he will whip up something in your price range." I went back to the committee and began work on Plan B!

Henry was perspicacious, which my dictionary defines as shrewd, perceptive, astute, clever, insightful, sage, aware, and discriminating. It was Henry's perspicacity that enabled him to be a visionary, capable of seeing beyond the traditional, hide-bound strictures of investing, and instead to underwrite ventures in Silicon Valley at a time when people did not know where or what that was! (This explains why Henry was always fond of the latest gadgets!)

So we gather this morning to commit to God's eternal care Henry Lea Hillman—philanthropist, industrialist, investor, builder, visionary, devoted husband, paterfamilias, Princetonian, patriot, and a child of God. His achievements caused one writer to pen: "The Hillman name has come to embody the highest ideals of contributing to the common good." To which we add: "Well done, good and faithful servant. Enter into the joy of the Lord."

Let us pray:

> Set our feet on lofty places;
> gird our lives that they may be
> armoured with all Christlike graces,
> pledged to set all captives free.
> Grant us wisdom, grant us courage,
> that we fail not man nor thee.

AMEN.

"It is well with my soul"—a Coda

Paul Joseph Ross (1941–2000)
Preached in Cálvary Church, Pittsburgh
20 June 2000

> In my father's house there are many mansions. (John
> 14:2)

WE HUMAN BEINGS HAVE a penchant for describing deaths in one
of two ways. Keeping in mind the Psalmist's declaration that a
lifespan should be threescore years and ten—and, if we are lucky,
fourscore—we deem the deaths of septuagenarians and octogenar-
ians to be timely. But we deem as untimely the deaths of those
whose lives fall short of that Biblical standard. So it is that we are
tempted to say that the death of Paul Joseph Ross is untimely. "He
was too young to die," some will say. Others comment that he had
so much more to offer, and would have, had he lived a little longer.
Still others point to virtuosos like Heifetz and Stern, whose artistic
skill matured and mellowed with age, and say that they would have
wished such good fortune for Ross. And so it goes. This morning,
I would ask that we reexamine our conventional wisdom. In the
first place, in the eyes of God, who reckons existence in eternities
and not decades, the difference between fifty-nine and, say, eighty-
seven is infinitesimal. Isaac Watts's hymn drives the point home:
"A thousand ages in thy sight are like an evening gone; short as the
watch that ends the night before the rising sun."[14] If that reasoning

14. Watts, "O God Our Help."

doesn't grab you, try this: instead of zeroing in on the quantity of life, giving people credit for longevity, let us learn to concentrate on the quality of life and give people credit for what they are able to accomplish, despite the limited time allotted to them. Jesus, it will be remembered, walked this earth for a mere thirty-three years. Martin Luther King was felled by a sniper's bullet nine months shy of his fortieth birthday.

By this measure, Paul's life was long and rich. It can be said of Paul what can be said of very few, that his life, his livelihood and his passion were all the same—music! He took great delight in making music, offering music, teaching music, living music. And no one can say of Paul Ross's music what the emperor is alleged to have said about Mozart's—that it was made up of "too many notes." To Paul Ross, who knew all too well the disadvantages inherent in black skin and economic deprivation, music could open doors. In a city whose residents seem reluctant to cross its many bridges, Paul believed that music could bring together people of disparate cultural and ethnic groups. In a town where languages are outward and visible signs of distinct ancestries, Paul saw music as a universal language capable of facilitating communication among people who might not normally talk to each other. In a town of jocks, Paul Ross, during his years of providing leadership for the Pittsburgh Symphonette, proved that young people could learn discipline, cooperation, and teamwork as much in the orchestra pit as on a hockey rink, baseball diamond, or gridiron. If indeed (according to an African proverb unabashedly purloined by Mrs. Clinton) it takes a village to raise a child, Paul Joseph Ross was an elder in that village whose inhabitants entrusted their children to his lavish attention and loving care.

My sisters and brothers, our lives are like symphonies, except that our final movements are more likely to be *andante* or even *largo*, instead of *allegro* or *presto*. So it was with Paul. He slowed down toward the end, the prognosis was discouraging. But to the astonishment of his physicians and to the delight of those of us who loved him, a miracle happened. Paul was one of the few parishioners with whom I had the pleasure of enjoying a lively conversation three days after administering last rites. He was his old self—perky, jocular, fun-loving, and gracious. But more to the point, he was grateful, grateful for this reprieve, an opportunity for amendment of life, an opportunity to have life once more and to have it abundantly. An opportunity to be with his family; an opportunity to putter around the kitchen; an opportunity to listen to his music. But it was not to last. A final infection set in and there was no miracle this time. At first I thought that this was some kind of cruel trick, to be given hope, only to have it taken away. But I underwent a theological version of an attitudinal adjustment. I realized that what God had done was to decide to end Paul's life with a coda. Now musically, a coda, literally a tail, is defined as "a closing section of a composition that is formally distinct from its main structure." That coda provided me with a moment of grace I shall never forget. I had the privilege of bringing communion to Paul at his home, his beloved Charlotta, little Matthew, and Sarah (in a lion costume) at his side. A serenity, calm, and peace enveloped us as we partook of the Body and Blood of Christ. Paul's face was beaming.

It was as if Paul had heard the words of Jesus in today's Gospel: "In my father's house there are many mansions. If it were not so, would I have told you that I go to prepare a place for you? And when I go and prepare a place for you, I will come again and will take you to myself, and where I am you may be also" (John 14:2–3). Paul departed this life with the blessed assurance that God had prepared a special place for him, where, even as we speak, he is sitting in the first chair of the celestial orchestra, formerly occupied by Mr. Paganini, performing Mozart's *Coronation Mass*. But in his private moments, I imagine that he is playing a plaintive obligato to accompany the words of an old hymn:

> When peace like a river attendeth my way,
> When sorrows like sea billows roll,
> Then whatever my lot, thou has taught me to say,
> It is well, it is well, with my soul.
> My sin—oh, the bliss of this glorious thought—

My sin—not in part, but the whole—
Is nailed to the cross and I bear it no more,
Praise the Lord, praise the Lord, O my soul.

And the heavenly chorus will take up the refrain:

It is well, it is well,
It is well, it is well with my soul.

Rest eternal grant unto Paul, O Lord, and let light perpetual shine upon him. May his soul and the souls of all the faithful departed, through the mercy of God, rest in peace. AMEN.

Bibliography

Abelard, Peter. "O What Their Joy." In *The Hymnal 1982*, 623. New York: Church Pension Fund, 1985.

Ackley, Alfred. "I Serve a Risen Savior." In *Lift Every Voice and Sing II*, 42. New York: Church Pension Fund, 1993.

Alford, Henry. "Ten-thousand Times Ten-thousand." In *The Hymnal 1940*, 590 New York: Church Pension Fund, 1961.

Bowie, James Russell. "O Holy City, Seen of John." In *Hymnal 1940*, 494. New York: Church Pension Fund, 1961.

Catholic Church. *The Order of Christian Funerals*. New York: Catholic Book, 1989.

Episcopal Church. "A Bidding Prayer." In *The Book of Occasional Services*. https://extranet.generalconvention.org/staff/files/download/21033.

Episcopal Church. "Commemoration of the Dead." In *The Book of Common Prayer*, 382. New York: Oxford University Press, 1979.

Henley, William Ernest. "Invictus." Poetry Foundation. https://www.poetryfoundation.org/poems/51642/invictus.

Hoffacker, Charles. *A Matter of Life and Death: Preaching at Funerals*. Cambridge, MA: Cowley, 2002.

Hooker, Richard. *The Laws of Ecclesiastical Polity*. Rev. ed. Oxford: Oxford University Press, 2013.

Hughes, Robert G. *A Trumpet in Darkness: Preaching to Mourners*. Philadelphia: Fortress, 1985.

King, Martin Luther, Jr. "Remaining Awake through a Great Revolution." In *A Knock at Midnight*, edited by Clayborne Carson and Peter Holloran, 201–224. New York: Time Warner, 2000.

Kipling, Rudyard. "If." In *Kipling: Poems*, 170–171. New York: Everyman's Library, 2007.

Leo, James R. *Exits and Entrances*. Bloomington, IN: XLibris, 2008.

Lyte, Henry Francis. "Abide With Me." In *The Hymnal 1982*, 662. New York: Church Pension Fund, 1985.

Martin, Richard B. *On the Wings of the Morning: Two Islands, One Church*. Garden City, NY: Diocese of Long Island, 2006.

Neale, John Mason. "Jerusalem the Golden." In *The Hymnal 1982*, 624. New York: Church Pension Fund, 1985.

"A Prayer for All Conditions of Men." In *The Book of Common Prayer*, 32. New York: Oxford University Press, 1928.

Schmitz, Barbara G. *The Life of Christ and the Death of a Loved One: Crafting the Funeral Homily.* Lima, Ohio: CSS, 1995.

Scott, Lesbia. "I Sing a Song of the Saints of God." In *The Hymnal 1982*, 293. New York: Church Pension Fund, 1985.

Van de Mark, Donald. *The Good Among the Great: 19 Traits of the Most Admirable, Creative, and Joyous People.* Sonoma, CA: Columbia Island, 2011.

Watts, Isaac. "O God Our Help in Ages Past." Hymnal.net. https://www.hymnal.net/en/hymn/h/607.

Willimon, William H. *Worship as Pastoral Care.* Nashville, TN: Abingdon, 1979.